VAT in the European Community

VAT in the
European Community

Alan Buckett

VAT Partner
BDO Binder Hamlyn

Butterworths
London, Dublin, Edinburgh, Munich
1990

United Kingdom	Butterworth & Co (Publishers) Ltd, 88 Kingsway, LONDON WC2B 6AB and 4 Hill Street, EDINBURGH EH2 3JZ
Australia	Butterworths Pty Ltd, SYDNEY, MELBOURNE, BRISBANE, ADELAIDE, PERTH, CANBERRA and HOBART
Canada	Butterworths Canada Ltd, TORONTO and VANCOUVER
Ireland	Butterworth (Ireland) Ltd, DUBLIN
Malaysia	Malayan Law Journal Sdn Bhd, KUALA LUMPUR
New Zealand	Butterworths of New Zealand Ltd, WELLINGTON and AUCKLAND
Puerto Rico	Equity de Puerto Rico, Inc, HATO REY
Singapore	Malayan Law Journal Pte Ltd, SINGAPORE
USA	Butterworth Legal Publishers, AUSTIN, Texas; BOSTON, Massachusetts; CLEARWATER, Florida (D & S Publishers); ORFORD, New Hampshire (Equity Publishing); ST PAUL, Minnesota; and SEATTLE, Washington

A CIP Catalogue record for this book is available from the British Library.

ISBN 0 406 50155 6

Typeset by Phoenix Photosetting, Chatham, Kent
Printed and bound in Great Britain by
Mackays of Chatham PLC, Chatham, Kent

Foreword

Europe stands at a turning-point. Its nation states are preparing to do away with their frontiers and to meld a set of national economies hitherto divided by manifold barriers into a single entity. In responding in this manner to the challenges of the world market, Europe is showing its determination to exploit the opportunities and advantages inherent in a large single European internal market. This economic integration will also enhance decisively Europe's importance and position in the world.

The time has come for Europe's citizens to reap the benefits of the single market. Moreover, Europe's industry and business must have a sound basis to be able to face harsh competition on world markets. Only in this way can their competitiveness be safeguarded. The economic joining together of the peoples of the twelve member states does not mean only economic advantages, substantial though they may be. It means greater potential for the advancement of Europe's citizens and more jobs. Furthermore, other aspects of life in the Community, as well as politics, are bound to be affected by the completion of the single market. Research and technology, a responsible attitude to the environment, the very basis of our lives, are but two examples. As Europe grows, it will be taking upon itself an obligation to reduce gradually the gaps which separate its regions and to help the less-developed regions to cope with the more determined competition the single market is sure to bring.

VAT is an important tool in the furtherance of the single market common to the twelve member states, allowing free circulation of goods and services between the different countries. There has been much debate on the proposals for VAT in the single market and much progress has been made.

We have to explain to our citizens and those who trade with them what the VAT changes will mean to them and what opportunities and possibilities they offer.

For this reason I greatly welcome initiatives like BDO Binder's being published by Butterworths. It provides valuable information on the current VAT regimes in each country, the proposals and other ideas for change and the progress to date. In summary, an important and useful contribution on one of the major issues of the internal market.

August 1990

Bouke Beumer
Chairman of the Economic
and Monetary Committee of
the European Parliament

Contents

Tables

Introduction

From 1 January 1993, Europe is to have a single internal market. This decision, taken by the twelve heads of state and government of the European Communities, is enshrined in a document – The Single European Act – which has the force of international law. The removal of all the formalities and the creation of a single internal market of 320 million people are acts without precedent in political and economic history. The result will be an economic zone with more inhabitants than the US and Canada together.

Number of inhabitants in millions

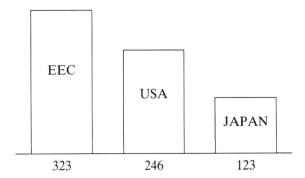

EEC	USA	JAPAN
323	246	123

Its gross domestic product of 3,856 bn ECU is almost as big as that of the US (3,950 bn ECU) and approximately twice the size of Japan's (2,097 bn ECU).

This market offers businessmen, workers and consumers, indeed all of Europe's citizens, a prospect of significant economic growth, better job opportunities, a rising standard of living and improved social conditions. But greater and more intense competition also

Gross domestic product in billions of ECU

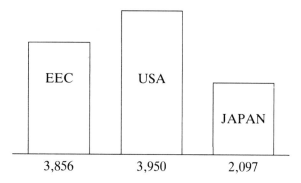

EEC	USA	JAPAN
3,856	3,950	2,097

means more challenges. Only those who can exploit the opportunities and challenges will reap the benefit of this massive political and economic undertaking.

Business has less than three years to prepare itself for a fundamental change in the economic climate in which it operates. Surveys have shown that the vital information is not circulating as widely as it should and yet that same information is a prerequisite for careful, detailed, advanced planning. As the proverb says, 'it is the early bird which catches the worm'. Company representatives and decision-makers, as well as those who have the task of devising strategies to maximise the opportunities and minimise the risks, will need both information and advice.

A plan to harmonise European Community (EC) rules and regulations and introduce common standards was proposed in the European Commission's white paper of June 1985. This suggested a series of approximately 280 legislative measures to achieve this objective by 31 December 1992.

The creation of a single internal market requires changes in all areas where different national laws, rules and regulations currently make it difficult for companies to operate freely. It is planned therefore to give priority to the removal of physical, technical and fiscal barriers. The term 'fiscal barrier' has come to apply to indirect taxes, that is, VAT and Customs & Excise duties, with direct taxation measures being considered under 'technical barriers'.

Of these three barriers, fiscal harmonisation may be the most difficult to achieve, not only because of the major differences between Community countries and fiscal policy, but also because of the domestic political effects that such changes are likely to have on individual voters within Community countries.

VAT is an important tool in the furtherance of the single market common to the twelve member states, allowing free circulation of goods and services between the different countries. VAT is payable by entrepreneurs on their receipts (output tax) and can be recovered by purchasers (input tax) who carry on an economic activity (business). In this way the burden of the tax is ultimately transferred to the final consumer.

However, although a common system of VAT is a requirement of the EC, there are still considerable differences in the application of VAT between the member states. As VAT is due on most supplies made for consideration, it is essential that potential transactions or business ventures involving EC countries are examined at as early a stage as possible so that suitable plans can be considered and penalties for non-compliance avoided.

This book, based on material written originally for the benefit of BDO clients and staff, is aimed at making entrepreneurs aware of their potential VAT liabilities when supplying goods or services in an EC country in which they are not established. It highlights the role of indirect taxes throughout the Community, the proposals for change, the problems which need to be overcome and the progress made up to 1 June 1990.

The book then explains, country by country, how each member state's VAT system operates as at 1 January 1990 under the following headings:

- Scope of the tax
- Rates of tax
- Tax invoices
- Place of supply
- Registration
- Importation procedures
- Input tax deduction
- Administration
- Appeals
- VAT and other taxes.

Each country's section is followed by an analysis of the procedure whereby VAT incurred in member states of the EC may be recovered by entrepreneurs registered for VAT in other member states or by taxable persons who are not established in EC territory.

Throughout the book the tax is referred to as VAT although each country has its own name and abbreviation for the tax as follows:

Belgium	Taxe sur la Valeur Ajoutee (TVA) or
	Belasting over de Toegevoegde Waarde (BTW)
Denmark	Mervaerdiafgift (MOMS)
France	Taxe sur la Valeur Ajoutee (TVA)
Germany	Umsatzsteuer (UST)
Greece	Foros Prostithemenis Axia (FPA)
Ireland	Value Added Tax (VAT)
Italy	Imposta sul Valore Aggiunto (IVA)
Luxembourg	Taxe sur la Valeur Ajoutee (TVA)
Netherlands	Belasting over de Toegevoegde Waarde (BTW)
Portugal	Imposto sobre o Valor Acrescentada (IVA)
Spain	Impuesto sobre el Valor Anadido (IVA)
UK	Value Added Tax (VAT).

Whilst every care has been taken to ensure that this book is factually correct (it states the position as at 1 January 1990) it is intended for general guidance only. As VAT legislation and administrative practices are constantly changing, readers are advised to seek professional guidance on any specific matters.

A D Buckett
VAT Partner
BDO Binder Hamlyn, UK
UK Representative and Secretary to the
BDO Binder Indirect Tax Committee

1 A guide to the EC proposals for change

AIMS AND ASPIRATIONS OF THE PROPOSALS

Harmonising indirect taxes within the EC was a principle embodied in the original Treaty of Rome which founded the Community in 1957. Some progress has already been achieved in that all member states have had to adopt VAT as their national sales tax and the Sixth Council Directive of 1977 provided for common definitions and a uniform basis for VAT. In addition, a proportion of the VAT base has become an element in the funding of the Community (known as 'own resources').

The EC Commission conceived that the decline of Europe relative to the rest of the world and particularly the US and Japan was due to the fragmentation of the European Market – still effectively twelve separate markets some thirty years after the Treaty of Rome. It is claimed that one of the factors contributing to a fragmented European market is the maintenance of Customs border controls. It is generally accepted that these barriers are costly ones for manufacturers and consumers alike.

In August 1987 the Commission brought forward a series of proposals which broadly involved:

- approximation of VAT rates by 1992;
- abolition of internal frontiers for VAT purposes by 1992 (ie charging VAT on exports of goods and services to other member states of the EC); and
- harmonisation of excise duties by 1992 (ie on hydrocarbon oils, tobacco, alcohol, etc).

VAT

The fiscal barriers which currently exist ensure than when goods cross internal frontiers, the correct revenue accrues to the right member state, with close checks on documents limiting the scope for fraud. Under the present system, tax is payable in the country in which the goods are ultimately consumed. An exporter receives a rebate of tax when he exports products, whilst the importer must pay tax on import. The essential feature of this system is that it is entirely dependent on frontier checks.

Without such border controls, it is claimed that the significant differences in VAT rates between neighbouring states would result in private consumers buying goods in a neighbouring state with a lower tax rate. It would also mean that businesses which could not recover all or some of the VAT they incur on purchases would be tempted to buy components and capital equipment across borders to save tax.

The startling effect to national governments with high VAT rates of removing frontier controls can be illustrated by the following examples:

Example: Current position

	Exporters effective VAT rate	*VAT due to Dutch government*
Components (value 100 ECU) produced in Holland and exported to Germany	0	0
		VAT due to German government
Components made into product (value 500 ECU) in Germany and exported to Denmark	0	0
	Effective VAT rate on sale	*VAT due to Danish government*
Product imported and sold by Danish retailer (value 1,000 ECU) to Danish consumer	22%	220 ECU

Example: Position if frontier controls abolished with no approximation of VAT rates

Effect

German producer may purchase components in Germany at 14% (100 × 14% = 14 ECU)*	Dutch supplier of components loses sale due to higher VAT rate (18.5%)
German producer sells direct to Danish consumer at 14% German VAT (1,000 × 14% = 140 ECU)	German government gains VAT revenue (140 − 14 = 126 ECU)
Danish consumer saves the difference between Danish and German VAT rates (220 − 140 = 80 ECU) by buying goods direct from Germany (possibly by mail order)	Danish government loses all VAT revenue

* Even though the German producer is able to recover Dutch VAT in this example he may prefer to purchase from a German supplier with a low VAT rate for cashflow and possibly other reasons.

Because of the distortion in tax revenues which would arise, the Commission argued that frontier tax controls could not be abolished without approximation of VAT rates, so as to ensure that cross-border shopping is unattractive and governments still maintain broadly similar VAT revenues. This is borne out by experience in the US which suggests that a difference of more than 5% in sales tax rates between states will inevitably lead to cross-border shopping.

Excise duties

Products such as alcohol, cigarettes, motor fuel, etc which are liable to excise duties, present similar problems with the difference in rates throughout the EC being even greater than the divergence in VAT rates. In addition, such rate differences are compounded by the addition of VAT in the importing state.

Because many products which are liable to excise duty are easy to transport, the Commission felt obliged to propose an average of the rates in force at 1 April 1987. The potential increase or decrease in a member state's revenue from the proposed excise duty changes, coupled with health factors on the taxing of alcohol and tobacco in certain states, were seen as presenting formidable problems in adopting the Commission's proposals in this area (see below page 16).

THE CURRENT POSITION

VAT

VAT rates throughout the EC vary between 0% and 38% with some countries having one single rate of VAT whilst others have up to six different rates for different products. The table below illustrates the wide divergence in rates in the EC. Several countries, most notably Ireland, Portugal and the UK, zero-rate a substantial number of domestically consumed products.

*VAT rates in the EC**

	Reduced %	Standard %	Higher %
Belgium	1 & 6	17 & 19	25 & 33
Denmark	None	22	None
France	2.1 to 13	18.6	25
Germany	7	14	None
Greece	3 & 6	18	36
Ireland	2 to 10	23	None
Italy	4 & 9	19	38
Luxembourg	3 & 6	12	None
Netherlands	6	18.5	None
Portugal (mainland)	8	17	30
(Madeira/Azores)	6	12	21
Spain	6	12	33
United Kingdom	0	15	None

* *Source: BDO Binder (at 1 April 1990)*

National laws versus EC laws

Notwithstanding such divergence in rates of VAT, all member states have to contend with challenges to their own domestic indirect tax laws from local taxpayers, other member states and the European Commission on the basis that the member states' enacted domestic law may not comply with the rules set out in the Council's Directives. An example of this can be seen in the UK where national laws have been over-ridden in court proceedings because of the primacy of EC law over national law. The UK has subsequently had to bring its national law into line with the EC law as set out in the Council's Sixth VAT Directive of 1977.

Of particular significance is the role of the EC Commission which monitors the implementation of the indirect tax regulations and directives and is not afraid of following challenges through to the European Court of Justice if member states refuse to co-operate. An example of this was the Commission's challenge of the UK and Irish Government's extensive use of zero-rating on a range of products, most notably new commercial construction, where the Commission was ultimately successful in 1988 and the relevant domestic law was amended in 1989.

Such moves by the Commission are seen as an attempt to ensure that all member states appreciate the importance of the common framework laid down by the directives and are seen as necessary steps in the removal of distortions between member states prior to the implementation of the 1992 frontier proposals.

Customs duties

One of the most significant stages in removing fiscal barriers was the abolition in 1968 of Customs duty in respect of trade between members of the European Community. In addition, under the auspices of the general agreement on tariffs and trade (GATT) reductions in general import duties were negotiated amongst industrial countries and this resulted in a general lowering of tariff levels on non-agricultural goods to the current 5%.

In addition, certain major changes were introduced on 1 January 1988 to simplify the operation of Customs duty formalities between member states. These changes included:

- the introduction of a single administrative document (SAD) which replaced some 100 existing national import entries and export declarations used by the member states of the EC;

- the introduction by the EC and other major trading nations of a new harmonised commodity and description coding system (HS);

- the introduction of an integrated tariff (TARIC), which brings together all the information about a product in a single reference.

However, it is the Commission's intention to do away with these controls at internal frontiers altogether.

Although the Treaty of Rome requires member states to pursue a common commercial policy towards trade with the rest of the world, most member states retain their own quantitative restrictions on certain imports (eg Japanese cars). In fact, Article 115 of the Treaty itself allows member states to monitor third country goods moving in free circulation across the Community. These restrictions must be eliminated by 1992; it is hoped the price will not be higher tariffs or the application of similar measures.

THE PROPOSALS

The following are the key proposals which are still to be adopted by the EC:

Harmonisation of turnover tax legislation

A number of proposals for directives have been produced by the Commission in recent years; those still outstanding include:

- **Proposal for a Twelfth VAT Directive** – This directive would require member states to limit the deduction of input tax on expenditure such as business travel, accommodation, entertainment, and the purchase, hire, repair and maintenance of passenger cars and pleasure boats. To date, member states have been unable to agree on the subject.

- **Proposal for a Sixteenth VAT Directive** – This proposal would avoid the double imposition of VAT on imports by private individuals from one member state to another. In a judgment in the European Court of Justice in the case of *Gaston Schul Duane Expediteur v Inspecteurde Invoerrectenen Accijnzen* 15/81 [1982] ECR 1409, [1982] 3 CMLR 229 it was held that the Netherlands, in making its own VAT charge on importation, must take into account the residual VAT already paid in the exporting state. This ruling has subsequently been implemented in most states and must eventually be adopted by all of them.

- **Proposal for a Nineteenth VAT Directive** – This proposal aims to clarify the rules in the Sixth VAT Directive on the definition of certain concepts such as 'means of transport', 'fixed establishment', the extent of certain exemptions and certain valuation rules. Following some amendments, the proposal is awaiting Council approval.

- **Proposal for a Directive on VAT Schemes for Small and Medium-sized Business** – This proposal aims to introduce a compulsory exemption from registration limit of 10,000 ECU (the current limit is 5,000 ECU) with an optional higher limit of 35,000 ECU). The proposal also aims to introduce simplified accounting procedures for businesses whose annual turnover is less than 200,000 ECU. Under such procedures VAT would be payable at the time of receipt of the payment instead of at the time of supply, annual tax returns would be introduced and member states could apply flat rate schemes. Little progress has been made with the proposal, although certain countries have received derogations under existing law to introduce simplified schemes for small and medium-sized businesses (eg cash and annual accounting).

Completing the VAT system

As part of the 1987 package for the removal of fiscal frontiers, the Commission proposed a directive under which, by 1992, all member states would apply a two-tier VAT rate structure, with a reduced rate of between 4% and 9% and a standard rate of between 14% and 20%.

The reduced rate would apply to basic necessities in the following categories:

- foodstuffs, excluding alcoholic drinks;
- energy products for lighting and heating;
- pharmaceutical products;
- water supplies;
- passenger transport;
- books, newspapers and periodicals.

This proposal replaces the standstill proposal on VAT and excise duties, which aimed at ensuring member states could not introduce new rates or rules which moved away from, rather than towards, the common structure envisaged by the Commission.

Removal of fiscal frontiers

As part of the 1987 package for removal of fiscal frontiers, a directive has been proposed which would amend a number of the provisions of the Sixth VAT Directive. The areas covered include the place of supply, the territorial application of VAT and the deduction of tax incurred from other member states, which would replace the Eighth Directive Refund Scheme currently in force. Under the proposal, derogations which have been introduced by member states under Article 28 (Transitional Provisions) of the Sixth VAT Directive would cease to apply on 31 December 1992 at the latest.

VAT clearing house

A 1987 Commission document outlined plans for a proposal to introduce a clearing house system. Under this proposal, output tax invoiced and collected on export sales in one member state would be reimbursed to the member state in which the recipient trader deducted input tax.

The clearing house system was to operate on the basis of VAT owed to or from a central EC VAT account, with the object of ensuring that the total VAT charged on goods continued to accrue to the country in which the exported goods were finally consumed. The system would have resulted in traders in each state having to complete two extra boxes on VAT return forms recording the output tax and input tax on intra-Community trade.

During the discussions on the 1987 proposals, this clearing system was seen as a serious problem by governments and businesses. Governments feared that it might not work properly and businesses feared that to correct its defects, heavy extra compliance burdens might become necessary.

To meet this problem, Madame Scrivener, the EC Commissioner for taxation, suggested that EC sales between group companies could be made free of VAT, which would have cut by about three-quarters the amount of money to be reallocated by the clearing house. For the sales on which VAT would still have to be paid it was suggested that statistics of intra-EC trade could be used to redirect the tax to the importing country.

On 9 October 1989, the EC Finance Ministers unanimously rejected the clearing house plan. They rejected the proposals regarding intra-group sales as too likely to lead to tax fraud and the use of statistics as unreliable. Whether the clearing house proposal is revisited in future years depends on whether the improvements proposed for the present system prove workable.

Convergence of VAT rates

Under the 1987 package on the removal of fiscal frontiers, this proposal (which replaced the 1985 proposal for a standstill directive referred to above) would prevent member states from altering the level and number of VAT rates at the date the directive was adopted. The proposal was aimed as a stop-gap until agreement was reached on the number and level of rates which should exist from 1992. The proposal would, however, allow those member states with three rates to reduce them to two (standard and reduced) and those states which apply only one rate to increase it to two (standard and reduced). Member states are also able to change the levels of their existing rates provided they move towards or within the two rate bands referred to on page 11, ie 4%–9% and 14%–20%.

MARKET AND SECTOR IMPLICATIONS

Given the many variables both within and outside the indirect tax system and the time gap between now and 1992, any overall estimate of the effects on market sectors can only be very imprecise.

On the basis of the 1987 proposals, analyses of current consumption and physical data suggested that of the existing twelve member states, Ireland and Denmark would incur significant budgetary losses from the proposed changes; Luxembourg, Spain and Portugal would make significant gains; Germany, Greece and the UK would make modest gains; France would incur a slight loss, and Belgium, Italy and the Netherlands would be in a fairly neutral position.

However, notwithstanding the budgetary effects, the social implications would be considerable. The UK and Ireland would have to charge VAT on goods which are currently zero-rated. Wine-producing countries such as Germany, Italy, Spain, Portugal and Greece would have to charge a duty on wine where there is none at present. Some member states would be faced with steep increases in their excise duties on alcoholic beverages and cigarettes, others would face considerable reductions.

The proposed changes in VAT and excise duty rates will undoubtedly influence the demand for products. In broad terms, it is to be expected that the charging of VAT on an item currently free of VAT or the increase in the rate of VAT on products will increase their price and so reduce the quantity purchased. However, this is an over-simplification, as the extent of such an effect will depend on the rate of VAT, how essential people consider the commodity to be and what proportion of their budget is spent on it.

In view of the fact that VAT and excise duty rates in some countries will increase under the 1992 proposals and decrease in others, all companies throughout the EC should be considering the potential indirect tax implications on future sales of their products and the effects on profitability. Planning strategies must then be developed to ensure that potential threats are recognised and, if possible, overcome and opportunities are acted upon as soon as possible. Any companies designing or purchasing new computer record systems will have to bear in mind the possibility of extensive amendments being required within the next few years.

Many businesses throughout the EC have been making representations both to their own national governments and to the EC Commission, and doubtless this trend will continue. There is also no doubt that whenever the proposals are adopted, in whatever form they finally appear, there are bound to be winners and losers.

PROGRESS TO DATE AND THE FUTURE ISSUES TO WATCH

Following much debate on the 1987 VAT proposals, the Commission put forward extensive revised proposals in May 1989. The revised proposals clearly tried to meet the principal objections to the original proposals, without sacrificing what the Commission saw as essential to the overall purpose of creating the single market.

The May 1989 proposals

The proposed rate band of 4%–9% for necessities was retained, but instead of a band of 14%–20% for the standard rate, what was proposed was a minimum standard rate of 15% with each state free to choose a higher rate if it wished. Furthermore, the modified proposals were to allow the UK to preserve some of its zero-rating on 'a very limited number of products'.

For businesses throughout the EC, a worrying feature of the 1987 proposals was the VAT clearing house (see above). Each government would refund to taxable traders foreign VAT they had paid on an import from another EC country and would then reclaim it from a central clearing house, which would be paid it by the government of the exporting country. Notwithstanding revised proposals in May 1989 for the clearing house system (see above) EC Finance Ministers remained opposed to the idea and in October 1989 rejected the plan.

Under the 1987 proposals, substantial diversions of trade to low rate countries could have been encouraged where the purchaser was not entitled to reclaim VAT. In May 1989, solutions were proposed for three important cases:

- exempt businesses and public institutions who purchased from other countries would have the VAT adjusted upwards or downwards so that it equalled the VAT they would have paid had they purchased in their own country;

- motor cars would be subject to VAT in the country where the purchaser registered them;

- mail order companies or traders who delivered goods to a customer in another country would charge tax at the rate applying in the customer's country.

These rules were thought necessary in these three cases to prevent differences in VAT rate affecting choice and to ensure that the tax is received by the customer's country and not the vendor's.

Following further discussions on the May 1989 revised proposals, the EC Finance Ministers at a meeting in October 1989 formally rejected the clearing house proposals. In their view the present system could be retained, but they shared the Commission's desire to abolish border controls. To meet this aim, they proposed a system of cross-checking traders' records after transactions to ensure that what had been zero-rated in the exporting country was duly taxed in the importing country.

In reply, the Commission questioned whether this proposal could be an adequate safeguard against error and fraud without becoming so great a burden on businesses as to negate the benefit of having abandoned border controls.

Following further discussions on the May 1989 revised proposals, the EC Finance Ministers at a meeting in October 1989 reached agreement that from 1 January 1993:

- the present system of taxing exported goods in the importing country will remain;

- the exporting country will refund to exporters VAT levied at previous stages;

- border checks will be abolished and will be replaced by administrative checks on traders' records to ensure that what has been zero-rated in the exporting country was duly taxed in the importing country;

- the clearing house proposal was formally rejected;

- private individuals will be permitted to purchase goods subject to VAT in one country without paying additional VAT in the other country. An exception will be made for motor cars and goods purchased through mail order businesses. For some EC governments this proposal would be acceptable only if VAT rates were approximated and there remains disagreement on what the approximated rate should be. A re-examination of the approximation of VAT rates at a future meeting was agreed;

- the modified proposal on excise duty rates, whereby there would be a minimum rate for each product, together with a higher target rate was accepted. It was also agreed that there will be a system of linked bonded warehouses for traders, so that goods may travel from one country to another without incurring duty and incur it only in the country where the goods are offered for sale to retailers or the general public. Goods will be physically marked to show what country's excise duty they have borne as a safeguard against goods being taken out of bond in a low-excise country and then offered for sale in a high-excise one. It will be an offence to sell goods with no mark or the wrong mark.

At a further meeting in December 1989, it was concluded that the Community should aim to reach a decision on standard rates of VAT by the end of 1991 either on the basis of a rate band or a minimum rate within a 14%–20% band. The UK still takes the view that Community decisions on tax rates are neither necessary nor desirable.

Summary

At 1 January 1990 agreement still had to be reached in the following areas:

Rate bands

- Will these be fixed by Community legislation or by natural deregulatory market forces?

- If the bands are fixed by Community legislation, will the reduced rate be as proposed (4%–9%)? What 'number of limited products' will still be eligible for zero-rating in home markets? Will this be limited to, in the UK for example, food and children's clothing, or will the whole of the UK's current zero-rating system survive intact? If not, will this mean VAT being levied on new houses, transport and goods sold by charities, etc?

Compliance burdens

- With agreement to abolish border controls, a system of post-transaction checks on exports and imports will have to be agreed which, on the one hand, represents a reasonably fraud-proof system and yet, on the other, is not as equally bureaucratic as border controls by means of close monitoring of traders' records. The decision to abolish border controls comes at a time of considerable discussion within the Community about high levels of fraud in areas such as the Common Agricultural Policy. Finance Ministers, aware of the risks, have agreed that machinery for international cross-checking may be needed, including liaison centres in each country and closer auditing of traders;

- Will the new system of cross-checking prove more cumbersome and produce more delays than border controls?

- Will a special form to accompany the goods be required?

- How will the new system apply in the case of motor cars, mail order traders and purchases from other countries by exempt and small traders?

- How will the new system deal with goods invoiced from one country to another but physically delivered to a third country?

- How much will the new system of international cross-checks on traders cost EC tax payers?

Review of the VAT system

In agreeing to retain the system whereby exports are taxed in the country of import, it was accepted that this system should be retained for a limited period only. One reason given for not adopting the Commission's proposals was that Finance Ministers felt there was insufficient time before 1992 to make all the detailed arrangements needed for switching to the Cockfield or Scrivener systems. They therefore agreed to proceed with their improvements to the present system, but to consider switching to another system following a review of the workings of the improved system after a few years. The Commission has shown an interest in this, provided that a firm date for making the changes is set. 1997 has been suggested as a possible date.

The May 1990 proposals

On 8 May 1990 the EC Commission announced its compromise proposals on how VAT should be collected after the abolition of border frontiers. The revised proposals, still to be discussed and agreed by the EC Finance Ministers, include the following points:

- Member states may continue to collect VAT until 1996 in the country where the goods are consumed, with goods zero-rated for export within the EC, as at present.

- The existing system of Customs checks would be replaced under the new scheme by fiscal controls designed to end the administrative burden on companies and yet provide effective checks against fraud.

- There would be no requirement for intra-Community trade to complete the Single Administrative Document (SAD), a form containing 54 questions which exporters have to complete for every consignment. It has been estimated that between 50 and 60 million SADs are used in purely intra-Community trade each year.

- For traders subject to VAT, the only obligations relating to intra-Community trade will be:

  — the inclusion in their normal periodic VAT returns of two global (import and export) figures for their trade with other member states;

  — the inclusion of the VAT number of seller and purchaser on the invoice documenting the transactions;

  — the obtaining of a declaration from the domestic VAT authorities that they are subject to VAT. This documentation would be given to the seller in the other country as a precondition for the zero-rating of exports.

- Large companies, meaning the 15% to 20% of EC companies that account for some 80% of Community trade, would also have to complete a monthly form requiring further statistical information.

- To help prevent fraud, member states would be responsible for collecting information about their own companies which would have to be submitted, on request, to other countries' tax authorities.

- Current VAT rates will not be directly affected, although Madame Scrivener, the EC Commissioner for taxation, has implied that greater intra-EC trade would allow market forces to have an effect in bringing VAT rates together.

- If accepted by EC Finance Ministers, the scheme based on the above proposals would run until 1996 when the EC Commission will wish to reconsider the adoption of its earlier proposal to charge VAT on exports coupled with a central clearing house to redistribute VAT revenues.

- The above proposals do not apply to excise duties but it is likely that when the Commission unveils its plans these will involve the establishment of a network of linked bonded warehouses throughout the EC.

2 The current position

As explained in the introduction (page 3), there are still considerable differences in the application of VAT between the member states; the basic rules which apply to each state are therefore set out in the following chapters.

Where two or more states are involved there may be a double charge to VAT, so there are schemes whereby VAT incurred in member states of the EC may be recovered by entrepreneurs registered for VAT in one member state or by taxable persons who are not established in Community territory.

Two such schemes exist:

- the Eighth Directive scheme which allows an entrepreneur registered for VAT in one member state to recover VAT incurred by him in another member state; and
- the Thirteenth Directive scheme which allows a taxable person who is not established in Community territory to recover VAT incurred by him in a member state.

The reasons for the existence of these refund schemes are set out briefly in this chapter together with those features of the schemes which are common to all member states.

The following chapters also provide a country by country analysis of the practical methods of refunding VAT in each country in connection with the schemes in the form of answers to a series of standard questions. These not only highlight those items of expenditure on which VAT may not be recoverable in a particular country, but also emphasise variations in the schemes between countries. Wherever possible, guidance is given to potential claimants on the practical pitfalls and planning opportunities which have been experienced when advising on and dealing with the schemes. This information will help to ensure that appropriate claims are dealt with efficiently by the relevant tax authorities and with the minimum of delay.

DEFINITIONS

There are a number of technical terms which are used throughout the following chapters and these are defined below. However, it is not necessarily the case that each member state has adopted all the VAT regulations or interprets them in the same way, so it is always best to check with the country concerned if there is any doubt.

Entrepreneurs (also called taxable persons)

Any person who independently carries out in any place an economic activity for the purpose of obtaining income, whatever the purpose or result of that activity. This covers all forms of taxable enterprises, including companies, partnerships, individuals and trusts. Since, in some cases, repayments are available to non-EC traders it has a broader meaning than 'VAT registered person'.

Taxable operation

- the supply of goods or services subject to tax;
- self supplies;
- the importation of goods.

Supply of goods

The transfer of the right to dispose of tangible property (essentially the sale of tangible property).

Supply of services

Any transaction which does not constitute a supply of goods is deemed to be a supply of a service.

The place of supply

Depending where the place of supply takes place VAT is due or not due.

- for tangible property, VAT is due in the country in which the delivery (transfer of title) takes place;
- for services, VAT is due in the country in which the supplier is established.

Zero-rating/exemption with credit

If supplies are exempt as a general rule it is not possible for a trader to reclaim (pro rata) any input tax in respect of them. However, in certain cases countries grant some supplies an exemption with credit so that credit can be taken for the input tax. This usually applies to exports of goods and some services linked to international trade. These supplies are often referred to as being taxable but at a zero-rate.

WHY THE REFUND SCHEMES ARE NECESSARY

A feature common to all the VAT systems throughout the EC is that generally the whole amount of VAT suffered on expenses incurred in the course of a business is recoverable. For an entrepreneur established in a member state this recovery normally takes place by offsetting the tax incurred against the tax due to the authorities. If tax recoverable exceeds tax due the entrepreneur will receive a refund from his member state's tax authorities.

This is best illustrated by the following example:

An entrepreneur is registered for VAT in the United Kingdom and supplies goods and services to the value of £95,000 in a calendar year. Not all the goods and services attract a positive rate of VAT, some being exempt, others being liable to VAT in principle but at a zero-rate.

VAT charged on supplies made:

	NET £	VAT £
Goods and services at standard rate (15% in UK)	80,000	12,000
Goods and services at zero-rate	15,000	Nil
TOTAL	95,000	12,000

VAT incurred on expenditure:

On goods and services at standard rate	60,000	9,000
On goods and services at zero-rate	10,000	Nil
	70,000	9,000

In effect the entrepreneur has charged and collected £12,000 of VAT which is payable to the tax authorities, but he is also entitled to recover from the authorities the £9,000 VAT which he has paid out on his expenditure. In practice the entrepreneur will credit the deductible tax against the tax due and remit only the balance, £3,000 in the above example, to the tax authorities. If deductible tax exceeds tax due, for example if a larger proportion of taxable supplies attracted no positive tax, the entrepreneur would reclaim the balance from the tax authorities.

Thus an entrepreneur who makes taxable supplies in a member state and who is registered in that state has always been able to take credit for or reclaim local VAT incurred in his own state. The refund schemes apply to VAT suffered in states where the entrepreneur is not registered in that state.

THE COMMUNITY ROLE

Before describing the salient features of the scheme it is worth noting the role played by the EC directives in introducing the facility to recover foreign VAT throughout the Community.

The First EC Directive on turnover taxes in the EC was issued on 11 April 1967 and introduced the obligation for all member states to adopt the value added tax system of indirect taxation. On 17 May 1977 the Sixth Directive, relating to harmonisation of VAT in member states, was issued and this introduced the concept of repaying VAT suffered by entrepreneurs in one member state on expenditure incurred in another member state.

On 11 January 1978 a draft Eighth Directive was tabled which required all member states to introduce the regulations as well as the law, where not yet in force, to allow VAT to be repaid on the basis proposed by the Sixth Directive. This Directive was adopted in Brussels on 6 December 1979 and required the regulations to come into general force on 1 January 1981. Many states had in fact repaid VAT in these circumstances for several years prior to 1981;

some indeed have not restricted repayments to entrepreneurs established in the European Community.

On 19 July 1982 a draft Thirteenth Directive was proposed which required all member states to introduce regulations and laws to allow VAT to be repaid to non-EC entrepreneurs. This Directive was adopted by the Community in Brussels on 17 November 1986 and required the regulations to come into general force on 1 January 1988.

HOW THE SCHEMES WORK

Under the Eighth Directive Refund Scheme an entrepreneur or trader who is registered for VAT in one member state, but who is not required to be registered in another, is able, subject to certain time and cash limits, to claim a refund of VAT on expenses incurred by him in member states in which he is not registered. Refunds are allowed only to the extent that such VAT would be deductible as input tax by an entrepreneur established in the member state from which a refund is being claimed.

Thus VAT cannot, in general, be reclaimed in respect of expenses incurred by an entrepreneur where his business by its nature would be treated as exempt if he were carrying it on in the country of the claim. An example of this would be VAT on expenses incurred by an insurance company representative in connection with supplies of insurance which are exempt in the country of the claim, regardless of the VAT treatment of such supplies in his own country.

It should be noted that refunds of foreign VAT cannot be claimed on the VAT returns which the entrepreneur submits to his own state's tax authorities. Special refund application forms, backed by original documents, are submitted to nominated authorities in the member states in which the foreign VAT was incurred.

Refunds under the Eighth Directive scheme are available only to registered entrepreneurs in the European Community. The scheme does not enable repayments to be made either to persons who are not registered for VAT or to persons who, although registered, have incurred foreign VAT in connection with their private, as opposed to their business, activities. Thus, a UK businessman, registered for UK VAT, may be entitled to reclaim French TVA incurred at a trade fair in Paris where he is exhibiting his goods, but will not be able to reclaim French TVA in connection with a private non-business holiday in the South of

France. Refunds are made to non-EC traders under the Thirteenth Directive scheme which complements the relief for double taxation available to Community traders under the Eighth Directive.

Under both directives, refunds are restricted by the rules of the individual member states and VAT incurred on the following will not be refunded by any member state:

- exported goods (the usual reliefs relating to exported goods apply);
- supplies to a travel agent, tour operator, etc for the direct benefit of a traveller other than the travel agent, etc or his employee.

TIME AND CASH LIMITS

The general rule is that claims which exceed a prescribed minimum should be made for a calendar year. However, claims may also be made for any period of longer than three months within the calendar year (an intermediate claim). In such cases the prescribed minimum figure is substantially higher in order to reduce the number of claims.

Where claims have been submitted during a calendar year and there are less than three months of the year remaining, a claim for the remainder of the calendar year may be submitted to complete the year. In such circumstances the minimum figure will be that for an annual claim and not the higher intermediate claim. The minimum figures for each country are included under the appropriate sections. They are subject to EC regulations and are therefore broadly similar.

Claims made during one calendar year from the United Kingdom tax authorities:

(3 month minimum: £130)
(Yearly minimum: £ 16)

	1989	
	£	
January	40	
February	30	
March	70	
	140	Repayment due £140

April	30		
May	50		
June	40		
		120	(below minimum limit of £130)
July		50	
		170	Repayment due £170
August	50		
September	–		
October	100		
		150	Repayment due £150
November	10		
December	12		
		22	Repayment due £22 (exceeds £16)

Claims for a refund of VAT incurred in a calendar year must be made by 30 June in the following year (ie in the above example by 30 June 1990 at the latest).

There is an absolute time limit for submission of claims which must be made not later than six months after the end of the calendar year in which the tax was incurred, subject to each authority's discretion to allow late claims to be accepted. As will be seen in the commentary sections, most countries require the claim to be *received* by their tax authorities before expiry of the six months deadline; certain countries allow claims provided they are *posted* before the expiry of the six months deadline. If claims are refused on the grounds that they are out of time it may still be possible to negotiate an extension with the relevant authorities.

HOW TO APPLY FOR A REFUND

A claimant may use a form printed in any of the Community official languages, as a standard design is used throughout the Community. However, it may help to avoid delays if the form relating to the relevant country is used. An example of the standard refund application form for the UK is reproduced at Appendix 1 (page 158).

Although any of the standard forms may be used, they must be completed in block capitals in the language of the member state to which the claim is to be sent. Thus a UK entrepreneur claiming refunds from France, Germany and Holland may use the standard UK version of the form or any other standard version printed in an official language, but the forms must be completed in French, German and Dutch respectively and the same would be true for a US entrepreneur.

Each claim form must be accompanied by original invoices, vouchers or receipts which show the supplier's name and address, the claimant's name and address, details of the goods or services supplied, the date of the supply, the cost of the goods or services and the rate and amount of VAT charged. The relevant authorities will stamp each document and, provided the claim is satisfactory, return them within one month of receipt.

A special certificate of status, proving that the claimant is registered for VAT at the time of the claim and issued by the tax authorities in the country where the claimant is registered, must be submitted with the applications for refund. A separate certificate of status will be required to send to each state from which refunds are being claimed, but where a state already holds a certificate of status another need not be produced for a period of one year from the date of its issue.

Claims may be completed and sent direct to the relevant tax authority by the entrepreneur or they may be prepared and submitted by an agent. Each member state has slightly different rules about the use of agents and these are referred to in the commentary section. The relevant authority in each state must make a refund within six months of receiving a satisfactory claim. The refund, which will be in the currency of the state making it, will normally be made by credit transfer which can be arranged either in the member state of claim or the entrepreneur's own state. Bank charges may be payable for the transfer and the charge may be deducted from the amount refunded.

A tax authority may refuse all or part of a claim but must state its grounds for so doing. A claimant may appeal against a refund to the appropriate authority in the member state concerned, but there is no provision for the entrepreneur's own VAT authorities to intervene. Any sum repaid as a result of an incorrect claim may be deducted from any subsequent repayments.

FRAUDULENT CLAIMS

All member states take a serious view of fraudulent claims. If a refund is obtained in a fraudulent or irregular manner a member state may recover the amount wrongly paid and impose penalties under its domestic legislation. Where an administrative penalty has been imposed, but has not been paid, the state concerned may suspend any further refund. Where a fraudulent application cannot be made the subject of an administrative penalty, the state concerned may refuse any further refund for a maximum of two years from the date of the fraudulent application.

In the case of EC entrepreneurs, the relevant tax authority may also seek to invoke the EC mutual assistance provisions whereby the entrepreneur's own tax authority may provide assistance to another state's tax authorities for the recovery of tax and penalties.

PRACTICAL POINTS

Organisations wishing to recover foreign VAT under the scheme should ensure that all employees visiting member states obtain valid tax invoices for supplies of goods and services received in connection with the business activities.

It is understood that the relevant tax authorities reject claims where the name of the person or company shown as customer on an invoice does not match the name of the entrepreneur shown on the certificate of status. To avoid delay you should instruct employees to ensure that the precise name as shown on the certificate of status is included in the address on invoices. If you are registered as a group registration the certificate of status should list all the companies included in the group.

Such invoices should be routed to a person who will be responsible for collating the invoices into member state categories and excluding any invoices for supplies on which the tax is non-deductible.

Before claims are submitted the organisation should ensure that sufficient certificates of status have been obtained to accompany the claim forms and claims should then be submitted according to the cash and time limits relevant to each country.

Particular problems which have arisen in the past include the following examples:

> A company in one country supplies goods to a customer in another country and the contract requires the goods to be fitted in the customer's country, such as the supply of an industrial furnace. Under EC rules this represents a supply of goods in the customer's country and will normally result in the overseas supplier having to register for and charge VAT in the customer's country. The use of the EC refund scheme for reclaiming VAT on, say, engineers' hotel expenditure will not normally be appropriate.

> A company or organisation established in one country may have representative offices in other countries. Although such offices may make no taxable supplies in that country they may be eligible to register for VAT on the basis that their purchases of goods and services result in them having business establishments in the relevant country. Again, the use of the VAT refund scheme described in this book would be inappropriate as VAT will be recovered by a VAT registration in the country concerned.

Organisations in either of these categories should be aware that the VAT treatment may vary from country to country and might be subject to concessionary treatment.

Country by country analysis

3 Belgium

SCOPE OF THE TAX

VAT was introduced into Belgium on 1 January 1971, replacing the old cumulative turnover taxes. The law of 27 December 1977 amended the VAT law, in order to bring the Belgian legislation into line with the requirements of the EC Sixth Directive.

VAT legislation consists of the Code (103 Articles), 41 Royal Decrees and 19 Ministerial Decrees and is implemented by administrative rulings.

The VAT code applies throughout Belgian territory.

VAT is administered by a department of the Ministry of Finance ('Administration de la TVA, de l'Enregistrement et des Domaines').

VAT is charged on:

- the supply of goods of a movable nature in Belgium by a taxable person (belastingplichtige – assujetti) in the course or furtherance of a business;
- the supply of services in Belgium by a taxable person in the course or furtherance of a business; and
- the importation of goods into Belgium by *any* person (not only a taxable person).

The supply of immovable property is generally exempt from VAT; however, in certain clearly defined cases VAT is charged on the supply of new buildings but the circumstances can be complicated and professional advice should be sought in this situation.

An entrepreneur for VAT purposes is anyone whose activity consists in effecting, in a regular and independent manner, with or without a profit motive, on a principal or an accessory basis, supplies of goods or services referred to in the Code.

There is no minimum turnover exemption for VAT registration purposes.

RATES OF TAX

The current standard rate of VAT is 19%.

Principal supplies	*Rate*
Gold for investment purposes	1%
'Vital necessities'	6%
Certain goods and services	17%
All other goods and services not dealt with elsewhere	19%
Luxury goods and motor cars	25%
Specified luxury goods and luxury cars	33%

Certain supplies of goods and services are exempt from tax but carry a zero rate, others are exempt from VAT altogether. The main types of *zero-rated* supplies are as follows:

- exports;
- certain international transport services;
- supplies of goods to embassies and certain international institutions; and
- supplies of services in Belgium by an agent with regard to operations located outside Belgium.

The main types of exempt supply are as follows:

- insurance;
- financial institutions;
- services by certain independent professions (eg lawyers' fees);
- education; and
- health.

TAX INVOICES

When a registered person supplies goods or services to another, he must issue a tax invoice. The recipient must retain this in order to reclaim input tax. Tax invoices must show the following:

- date of issue;
- serial number;
- supplier's name, address and VAT number;
- customer's name and address;
- date of supply;
- a clear description of the goods or services supplied including

  — information required to determine the applicable rate of
  tax,
  — quantity of goods supplied,
  — price,
  — rate of tax, and
  — total tax chargeable.

Unless the law states otherwise, a taxpayer supplying goods or services to individuals who do not intend to use them for business purposes is exempted from this invoicing requirement.

Less detailed invoices can only be issued for a supply of petrol below Bfr 2,500.

PLACE OF SUPPLY

The application of Belgian VAT is limited to transactions within Belgium. It is important in order to determine the place of supply of goods to determine the time of supply. Then, the place where the goods are located at that time must be determined. If this is Belgium, Belgian VAT will be due. If it is outside Belgium, no Belgian VAT will be due, even if the transaction is concluded between two entrepreneurs who are resident in Belgium.

Supplies of goods

Generally, the time of supply is the time at which the goods are placed at the disposal of the acquiring party or transferee.

Special rule for transportation

If a supply requires transportation of the goods, it is deemed to occur at the moment such transportation commences.

Example

> 'A', established in France, sells merchandise stored in city F in France to his customer in city B in Belgium. Under his sales contract, the supplier is required to deliver the goods in city B. Consequently, supply takes place at the time transportation commences in France and no Belgian VAT is due on the transaction. Note, however, that VAT will be due because the goods are imported into Belgium.

If a supply requires both the transportation and installation or assembly of the goods transported, the supply is deemed to occur at the moment the installation or assembly is completed.

Example

> If, in the above example, the supplier is also required to assemble the goods in city B, the supply takes place at the time of the completion of the assembly. Since at that time the goods are located in Belgium, Belgian VAT is due on the transaction.

There are special administrative rules and permits required when transportation and installation are effected by a non-resident entrepreneur who does not have a permanent establishment in Belgium.

Supplies of services

A supply of services is only subject to Belgian VAT if the supply:

- takes place in Belgium;
- is effected by an entrepreneur in the course of his business; and
- is not exempt from tax.

The place of supply of services is determined on the basis of non-refutable legal presumptions. There are four special criteria and one general criterion. Depending on the type of service, the following criteria are used:

- the place where the goods are located;
- the place where the service is executed;
- the place where the service is used;
- the place where the customer is located.

If none of these criteria is applicable, the general rule applies (ie the place where the supplier is established).

If a non-resident entrepreneur supplies a service for a Belgian customer, the above criteria must be used to determine whether the service is rendered in Belgium. If this is the case, the principle is that the non-resident entrepreneur must register with the VAT authorities prior to supplying the service. A number of exceptions are, however, provided in this respect (for example occasional supplies, intellectual services and so on).

REGISTRATION

Generally, the VAT provisions applying to resident entrepreneurs apply also to foreign, non-resident entrepreneurs. Non-resident entrepreneurs who have a permanent establishment in Belgium are treated in all respects like resident entrepreneurs. But non-resident entrepreneurs who do not have a permanent establishment are required to appoint a responsible representative in Belgium.

A permanent establishment for the purposes of VAT is defined as a place of management, a workshop, an agency, a warehouse, an office, a laboratory, a sales or purchasing office, a depository or any other fixed installation excluding, however, a building site. Moreover, in order for a non-resident entrepreneur to register a permanent establishment he will have to prove that he is an entrepreneur within the meaning of the Belgian VAT code and the permanent establishment must be managed by a person who can enter into binding legal contracts with clients or customers on behalf of the non-resident entrepreneur. However, it is not necessary that this person resides in Belgium or has Belgian nationality. Accounts must be kept at the permanent establishment and the establishment must supply goods and/or services as provided in the Code.

Non-resident entrepreneurs carrying on construction or assembling activites in Belgium do not have, per se, a permanent establishment in Belgium for VAT purposes, irrespective of the duration of time or number of assembly points involved. They should register themselves in Belgium as entrepreneurs in the building industry if their activities within Belgium relate to immovable property. They may, however, have a permanent establishment for income tax purposes.

A group of companies must register each company separately even if owned or controlled by a single person.

IMPORTATION PROCEDURES

For the purposes of VAT, importation means the introduction of goods into Belgian territory.

Imports must be declared, at the frontier Customs control, as being intended for consumption, transhipment, storage in a bonded warehouse, or temporary exemption. If the goods are declared as being intended for consumption, payment of VAT is effected by the 'addressee' of the imported goods (ie the person that imports them). The importer is the recipient or transferee, or if there is no transfer, the proprietor of the goods.

The seller may also act as importer provided he has a permanent establishment or a responsible representative in Belgium. This may be necessary if the seller does not want to reveal to his customers who his supplier is (the import documents will list where the goods come from). In that case, however, the VAT law provides that the supply by the seller to the purchaser is taxable in Belgium.

Generally, the VAT on importation is paid at the time the goods transfer across the frontier Customs control. There are special regimes which make it possible to delay paying the tax when crossing the Customs control, and move the payment to the next tax return due from the addressee after importation. These special regimes are only applicable if the importer is a taxpayer who is subject to filing VAT returns.

For importations into Belgium from the Netherlands or Luxembourg, the special regime is only allowed in the following situations where:

- importation of the goods takes place pursuant to a contract concluded with a person who is established in Benelux, or if the goods were forwarded from a permanent establishment of the taxpayers in the Netherlands or Luxembourg;

- the goods are not under a special Customs regime permitting their VAT exempt import (for example goods designated for transit; goods imported under the TIR or ATA regime, etc); and

- the goods have been declared to the Customs offices indicated by the Minister of Finance.

For importations from other countries a similar regime is available if permission is granted by the Ministry of Finance and an amount of VAT is paid as guarantee.

INPUT TAX DEDUCTION

The right of deduction for input tax is complete and immediate except for VAT related to motor cars. In principle all input tax (including tax on investments) on purchases made during a tax period can be credited when the tax due for the period is calculated. However, there is no right of deduction when the input tax is related to exempt turnover. In these circumstances the input tax is a real cost for the enterprise and may be passed on to the next stage of turnover as a cost element in the price. Only 50% of the VAT on motor cars is reclaimable and VAT incurred on certain specified goods and services such as entertainment expenses, alcoholic beverages and so on is non-deductible.

ADMINISTRATION

The VAT authorities and the Land Registry in Belgium form one department of the Ministry of Finance.

VAT taxpayers with a permanent establishment in Belgium come under the VAT control authority for the area in which their establishment is located. VAT taxpayers without a permanent establishment fall under the Central VAT Office for Foreigners.

APPEALS

Any disputes over VAT rulings are settled by the ordinary courts as there are no specific VAT courts.

VAT AND OTHER TAXES

A person who cannot recover input tax, for example because he makes only exempt supplies, can treat the irrecoverable VAT element as part of the cost for other tax purposes. This applies also to those registered persons who because of partial exemption may only be entitled to partial VAT recovery.

VAT REFUND PROCEDURES

Entrepreneurs resident in the European Community

1 **Can a claim for a refund be made by the entrepreneur direct to the Belgian tax authorities?**
Yes. A claim can either be made directly by the non-resident entrepreneur or by his duly authorised agent.

2 **To what address should the claim be made?**
Centraal BTW Kantoor voor Buitenlandse Belastingplichtigen
Van Orleystraat 15
1000 Brussel.

3 **Which form should be submitted and in which language should it be completed?**
Belgian VAT form 821 should be used. This can be obtained from the above address. Any of the other standard forms used throughout the EC can be used instead. The form must be completed in Dutch, French or German (not in English). Form 803 (see question 11) should be used whenever a claim for the refund of Belgian VAT does not satisfy all the conditions for refund as set out for EC entrepreneurs.

4 **What are the minimum amounts that may be reclaimed and how frequently can such claims be submitted?**
The general rules relating to time and cash limits are set out in the introduction. The minimum amounts that may be claimed from the Belgian authorities are as follows:

	Minimum claim BFr
Calendar year claim	1,100
Intermediate claim	9,000
Claim for remainder of calendar year	1,100

No more than one claim can be submitted in any quarter.

5 **What is the time limit for submitting a claim?**
As a rule, the claim must be made within six months of the end of the calendar year but, in practice, claims made within five years of the taxable event may still be accepted.

6   Is any Belgian VAT not reclaimable?
In general, VAT cannot be reclaimed in respect of expenses incurred by an entrepreneur if his business would be treated as exempt were he carrying it out in the country of the claim. Nor can VAT be reclaimed if it relates to expenditure on tobacco, alcohol, restaurants and entertaining. Only 50% of the VAT on motor cars is reclaimable.

7   Which documents must be submitted with the repayment claim form?
The official claim form must be accompanied by the original invoices and a certificate of status, obtained from the claimant's own tax authorities to prove that the claimant is registered for VAT in a member state.

8   How long, on average, will the authorities take to repay the amount claimed?
A refund must be made within six months of receiving a satisfactory claim. In practice, however, claims are frequently not repaid within this limit.

9   Is it necessary to appoint a fiscal representative in Belgium and, if not, is it advisable to do so?
Claims may be made directly by the non-resident entrepreneur. Although there is no requirement to appoint a Belgian agent to submit claims, a person so appointed may well be able to assist in preparing proper claims and obtaining refunds as quickly as possible.

Entrepreneurs not resident in the European Community

10   Does the ability to make a claim also apply to non-EC entrepreneurs?
Yes. There is no restriction. An entrepreneur registered for business purposes in a non-EC country can use the scheme to reclaim VAT paid in Belgium, provided there is no other way of refunding VAT paid in Belgium such as by means of an agent responsible for VAT or an establishment registered for VAT purposes.

11   Is the procedure the same as for entrepreneurs resident in the EC?

The procedure is almost exactly the same as for entrepreneurs resident within the EC. However, the claimant must use Belgian VAT form 803. This can be obtained from:

Centraal BTW Kantoor voor Buitenlandse Belastingplichtigen
Van Orleystraat 15
1000 Brussel.

4 Denmark

SCOPE OF THE TAX

Denmark was one of the first countries to introduce VAT. The original Act No 102 of 31 March 1967 has been amended several times and the VAT rate has gradually been increased from 10% to 22%.

Initially, the tax concerned only goods and a limited number of services rendered. Now, however, following the amendment of 1 October 1978 (adopted under the EC Sixth VAT Directive – VAT) the tax is levied on all products (goods) and nearly all services.

For VAT purposes Denmark comprises only Denmark while Greenland and the Faroe Islands have their own VAT law. The Copenhagen Freeport has no VAT.

VAT is charged on:

- the supply of goods or services in Denmark which is a taxable supply; made by a taxable person; in the course or furtherance of a business;
- the import of goods into Denmark by any person (not only a taxable person); and
- the import of certain types of services into Denmark by a taxable person.

The word 'supply' is not defined but it encompasses all types of supply, sale, hire-purchase, hire, gift, loan, exchange, and so on. Certain transactions are deemed to be supplies, some even to be self-supplies; others are deemed not to be supplies. The distinction between whether a supply is one of goods or one of services is important because the rules governing the time and place of supply are different and, on occasions, it may decide whether the supply is taxable or not, or taxed at a zero rate.

Purchases and sales of real estate and letting of houses or apartments are not liable to VAT.

A 'taxable person' is any person (individual, partnership, company, foundation, club, association, charity, and so on) who is registered for VAT or is required to be registered. A person is obliged to register if, at any time, there are reasonable grounds for believing that the value of his taxable supplies in the period of one year from that time will exceed DK 10,000.

In broad terms 'business' means any activity, including any trade, profession or vocation, carried on with a reasonable degree of continuity and organisation, whether profitable or profit-making or not, which will exclude a hobby or the provision of services by an employee to his employer.

RATES OF TAX

The current standard rate of VAT is 22%. Certain supplies of goods and services are taxable but carry a zero-rate, others are exempt from VAT altogether.

The main types of *zero-rated* supplies are as follows, although it should be noted that there are many exceptions:

- food;
- books and newspapers;
- certain international services.

Services are excluded only if mentioned in the Act.

The following are the main types of exempt supplies although there are many exceptions:

- health services;
- medical and social services;
- education (vocational training);
- cultural activities (not including theatres, concerts, etc);
- sporting activities, especially when performed by amateurs;
- conveyance of passengers (apart from other commercial passenger transport by bus other than by regular service);
- postal services (apart from telecommunications);
- management of real estate, such as letting and leasing (not including letting of rooms in hotels, inns, etc);

- insurance transactions and bank and financing activities;
- lotteries, etc;
- literary and musical as well as other artistic activities;
- travel agencies and information activities, etc of tourist offices;
- services performed by undertakers, etc in direct connection with funerals.

Exports are free (ie zero-rated) from VAT in order to make VAT a domestic tax. This exemption is an exemption with credit. The enterprises do not include export sales in their taxable sales but are nevertheless entitled to deduct tax on purchases to the full extent.

Enterprises exporting the greater part of their production have a greater input tax than output tax during a tax period, and at the end of each period they will consequently have a claim on the Customs authorities for reimbursement of the amount of the difference. Such enterprises can obtain a tax period of one month and in special circumstances an even shorter period so long as it is not less than one week.

The Danish tax covers deliveries of all movable goods including secondhand goods. Ships of not less than five gross tons and aircraft are exempt. Sales of newspapers are also exempt. These exemptions may be regarded as zero rates, because shipyards and publishers are entitled to deduct input tax although no tax is collected on their sales.

TAX INVOICES

When a registered person supplies goods or services to another, he must issue a tax invoice. The recipient must retain this in order to reclaim input tax. Tax invoices must show, inter alia:

- VAT registration number;
- serial number;
- tax point;
- supplier's name and address;
- customer's name and address;
- type of supply;
- rate of tax; and
- total tax chargeable.

If the customer agrees, a less detailed invoice for supplies not exceeding DK 200 in value may be issued.

PLACE OF SUPPLY

A supply of goods/taxable services is treated as taking place in Denmark if the supplier 'belongs' in Denmark. An entrepreneur is treated as belonging in Denmark if he has a business or some other fixed establishment in Denmark, such as an office, showroom, factory or mobile workshop. If a business is carried out in Denmark through a branch or agency, the entrepreneur will be regarded as having a business establishment in Denmark.

If the entrepreneur has business establishments in more than one country and supplies services, each supply made will be looked at separately and the entrepreneur will be regarded as belonging in the country where the establishment is located which is most closely concerned with the particular supply.

Foreign residents who supply goods/taxable services in Denmark but have no establishment will be within the scope of Danish VAT. For example, an estate agent from outside Denmark who comes to Denmark and conducts his business from an office in Copenhagen would be regarded as belonging in Denmark in respect of those services.

When selling goods or services subject to taxation the registered enterprise must collect VAT at 22%. The tax must be collected regardless of whether the enterprise sells the goods or renders services to a consumer or to another registered enterprise.

REGISTRATION

All enterprises carrying on independent commercial business with goods or taxable services must be registered with the Customs authorities. Only enterprises selling goods and taxable services up to an amount of DK 10,000 a year are not liable to pay VAT or to be registered.

Where two or more Danish companies resident in Denmark are under common control they may elect to be registered as a single group for VAT purposes so that transactions between members of the VAT group are ignored and only one VAT return is made by the group.

Some companies which are not liable to be registered and pay VAT can nevertheless apply to be registered.

The tax owed to the Treasury by registered enterprises is calculated quarterly. It is calculated as the difference between the tax collected (output tax) and the tax paid to suppliers and on imports (input tax). According to the ordinary procedure for industrial and trading enterprises, returns must be submitted by taxable enterprises within one month and 20 days from the end of each tax period, and tax liable for the period must be remitted at the same time.

If at the end of a quarter the input tax exceeds the output tax for the period, the enterprise in question will receive a reimbursement of the difference from the Customs authorities. Normally the refund will be made within three weeks after the receipt of the return for the period concerned.

Enterprises registered as farming, fishing and related activities submit returns only twice a year, each comprising six months, and the tax for each six months period is paid by two equal instalments in the sixth and the ninth month following the end of the tax period.

IMPORTATION PROCEDURES

Imported goods are taxed at importation, and the same rate is applied as on inland transactions – 22% of the taxable value. According to a system of deferred payment, importers pay the tax on goods imported during each month by the end of the following month. The tax on imports is calculated on the basis of the Customs value plus Customs duty and any other indirect taxes – payable in connection with the importation. When calculating the tax liable in a certain tax period the importer is entitled to deduct tax on goods imported in that period from the tax on sales.

Foreign enterprises which carry on independent commercial sales of goods or render services in Denmark on a permanent basis must be registered with the Customs authorities. If the enterprise has no branch or office in Denmark, it must be registered by a person resident in Denmark or an enterprise having a business office there.

A person operating an enterprise on his own account as owner, lessee or the like is liable for payment of the tax levied. Several enterprises which have common owners may elect for a system of joint registration, and they are consequently liable for the tax in respect of all the enterprises covered by the registration , and also for import VAT. When a foreign enterprise has been registered by a local representative, this representative and the undertaking will be jointly and severally liable for tax.

INPUT TAX DEDUCTION

The right of deduction for input tax is full and immediate. In principle all input tax on purchases – including tax on investments – made during a tax period can be credited when tax liable for the tax period is calculated by the enterprise. However, there is no right of deduction when the input tax is related to a non-taxable turnover (exempt supplies) and a person who makes only exempt supplies is not entitled to register and cannot therefore claim any VAT as input tax. Under these circumstances the pre-tax is a real cost for the enterprise and might be passed on to the next stage of turnover as a cost-element in the price.

There are some minor exemptions to the right of deduction. Deductible input tax does not include tax on:

- meals for the enterprise's owner and employees;
- acquisition and use of housing accommodation for the enterprise's owner and employees;
- remuneration in kind of the employees;
- acquisition and operation of creches, kindergartens, recreation centres, holiday homes, summer cottages, etc for employees;
- entertainment expenses and gifts;
- hotel accommodation; or
- acquisition and operation of passenger motor vehicles adapted for transportation of not more than ten persons.

Enterprises selling taxable as well as non-taxable services are entitled to a partial deduction of input tax corresponding to the relation between the transactions in the two branches of the enterprise (pro rata rule).

The normal rule is that possession of a tax invoice is essential to substantiate a claim to deduct input tax (that is VAT incurred on business expenditure). Only the person to whom the supply is made is entitled to claim input tax deduction; this may not necessarily be the person who pays for the supply.

ADMINISTRATION

The Treasury has overall charge of the imposition, regulation and collection of VAT in Denmark. However, whereas direct taxes (for example corporation tax and income tax are administered by the Inland Revenue), VAT is administered by the Customs and Excise. There are automatic, and in some cases severe, financial penalties in the VAT system to speed up the collection of VAT and increase the accuracy of the details on VAT returns.

APPEALS

A person may appeal against a decision by Customs and Excise if it falls within certain defined categories. Appeals are heard by independent VAT Tribunals in the first instance but may then proceed to the judiciary.

VAT AND OTHER TAXES

A person who cannot recover input tax, for example because he makes only exempt supplies, can treat the irrecoverable VAT element as part of the cost for other tax purposes. This applies also to those registered persons who may only be entitled to partial VAT recovery due to partial exemption.

VAT REFUND PROCEDURES

Entrepreneurs resident in the European Community

1 Can a claim for a refund be made by the entrepreneur direct to the Danish VAT authorities?
Yes. The claim may be made direct by the non-resident person or his appointed agent.

2 To what address should the claim be made?
Distriktstoldkammer 6
Stodsborgvej 303
2850 Naerum.

3 Which form should be submitted and in which language should it be completed?
The claimant may use the DK form R 861 obtainable from the address above. The form must be completed in Danish. Refund of VAT is described in booklet Y64 which is translated into English, German and French.

4 What are the minimum amounts that may be reclaimed and how frequently can such claims be submitted?
The general rules relating to time and cash limits are set out in the introduction. The minimum amounts which may be claimed from the Danish authorities are as follows:

	Minimum claim
	DK
Calendar year claim	200
Intermediate claim	1,500
Claim for remainder of calendar year	200

5 What is the time limit for submitting a claim?
The claim must be made and received by the Danish authorities not later than 30 June following the end of the relevant calendar year.

6 Is any Danish VAT not reclaimable?
As explained in the introduction, VAT cannot, in general, be reclaimed in respect of expenses incurred by an entrepreneur where his business would by its nature be treated as exempt if

he was carrying it on in the country of the claim. VAT is also non-deductible on certain business entertainment expenses.

7 Which documents must be submitted with the repayment claim form?

The official claim form must be accompanied by the original invoices and a certificate of status, obtainable from the claimant's own tax authorities, proving that the claimant is registered for VAT in the state where he is domiciled.

8 How long, on average, will the authorities take to repay the amount claimed?

The authorities must make a refund within six months of receiving a satisfactory claim. In practice, claims are repaid well within this limit. If a claim is not satisfactory, delays will occur whilst enquiries are made of the claimant.

9 Is it necessary to appoint a fiscal representative in Denmark and, if not, is it advisable to do so?

Claims may be made direct to the Danish tax authorities at the address above by the non-resident claimant or his non-resident appointed agent. Although there is no requirement to appoint a Danish agent to submit claims, an agent may well be able to assist in preparing proper claims and obtaining refunds as quickly as possible.

Entrepreneurs not resident in the European Community

10 Does the ability to make a claim also apply to non-EC entrepreneurs?

Yes. An entrepreneur registered for business purposes in a non-EC country can use the scheme to reclaim VAT paid in Denmark.

11 Is the procedure the same as for entrepreneurs resident in the EC?

Yes. The procedure is the same for entrepreneurs not resident in the EC as for those resident in the EC.

5 France

Since the First World War, there have been a variety of turnover taxes, which proved to be of help when it came to instituting a general tax on consumption in the EC.

From 1936 to 1967, VAT (called 'Taxe à la production' from 1936 to 1951) was due on the activities performed by producers, ie manufacturers. On 1 January 1968, in order to comply with the EC First and Second Directives, VAT was extended to operations performed in the course of industrial and commercial activities and the legislation was further amended with effect from 1 January 1979 in accordance with the Sixth EC Directive.

The French territory within which the tax applies comprises France and its territorial waters, Monaco and Corsica. It does not include Andorra. The French overseas departments are treated as export territories, and VAT applies in Martinique, Guadeloupe and Reunion at special reduced rates but it does not apply at all either in French Guyana or in Saint-Pierre-et-Miquelon. Similarly, VAT does not apply in the French overseas territories, which are also treated as export territories.

VAT applies to:

- the supply of goods or services made in France for consideration, when such a supply is made by a taxable person in the course or furtherance of an economic activity;
- the importation of goods into France by any person (not only a taxable person);
- self supplies; and
- certain purchases from non-taxable persons.

VAT also applies to new buildings but the rules are complex.

For the purposes of the tax a taxable person is one who independently carries out any economic activity, whether on an occasional or habitual basis, whatever the purpose or results of that activity and whatever the situation of that person with regards to other taxes.

Entrepreneurs liable to the tax must make monthly returns. Any late payment gives rise to a penalty of 0.75% for each month until the payment is actually made.

There are special rules for small entrepreneurs: if the amount due per year does not exceed 1,350 FFr, VAT is not levied. This corresponds to a taxable turnover of 8,600 FFr for operations liable to VAT at the normal rate of 18.6% and 20,600 FFr for operations taxable at the reduced rate of 5.5%. Where the amount of VAT due per year is between 1,350 FFr and 5,400 FFr there is a partial tapering of the amount due. The accounting formalities and filing obligations are also simplified for smaller businesses.

RATES OF TAX

The current standard rate of VAT is 18.6%.

Principal supplies	*Rate*
Reduced rate	5.5%
Most food for human consumption	
Medicines	
Some products	
The letting of furnished dwellings	
Public transport	
Books	
Certain products needed in agriculture	
Land for building purposes	13.0%
Standard rate	18.6%
All supplies of goods and services in France except those which are taxable at other rates or exempt.	

Luxury rate   25.0%
Luxury goods including cars, furs, jewels, records,
record players, cameras and 'pornographic' goods and
services.

Newspapers and journals are subject to 2.1% when published on a
daily basis, otherwise a rate of 4% applies.

Certain operations although falling within the scope of VAT are
exempt because of particular stipulations of the law. The main
exemptions are:

- health, medical and social services;
- most financial operations;
- insurance;
- the letting of unfurnished property;
- tuition and teaching;
- certain professional activities;
- writers and artists; and
- some charitable operations carried out by non profit-making
  bodies.

It should be noted that there are numerous exceptions to these
broad headings; for example certain financial transactions can be
liable to VAT if the taxpayer makes an election to pay the tax.

Exempt operations do not give rise to any deduction, whereas
exemptions relating to exports are zero-rated. French law does not
recognise zero-rated operations apart from exports. Exporters can
buy the goods that they require for export without paying VAT.

TAX INVOICES

The invoices delivered by taxable persons must bear the following
information:

- the name and address of the taxable person;
- the name and address of the client;
- the net price before tax of each unit sold or supplied;
- the total quantity sold before tax;
- the rate applicable to each product or services supplied;
- the total amount due before tax;

- the total VAT due.

The recipient must keep the invoice in order to reclaim input tax.

PLACE OF SUPPLY

The distinction between whether a supply is one of goods or one of services is important because the rules governing the time and place of supply are different and, on occasions, it may decide whether the supply is taxable or not, or taxed at a zero or positive rate.

Supplies of goods

The place of supply of goods depends on where the transfer of title takes place. If such a transfer takes place outside France, the supply is not taxable.

If it takes place in France, it is taxable; for example, if a US company exports products to be processed in France in order to sell them there after processing, it will be deemed to make a taxable delivery in France, though it may not have any establishment in France.

Again, if the US company buys products in France in order to resell them the resale is taxable in France. However, when a foreign supplier installs goods in France, the supplier is liable to French VAT on the delivery. Unlike the situation which exists in certain other EC countries, the foreign supplier cannot escape from paying the tax on the delivery of the goods, once installed, and recovering the input tax suffered on importation and on the expenses eventually incurred in France for that operation.

Supplies of services

The general rule is that a supply of services is taxable in France when the supplier is established in France, whether it be his main place of business or a fixed establishment from which the services are supplied. An office or a showroom will be sufficient. The purpose of the law is to charge the taxable supplier at the place where he supplies the services.

Exceptions to the rule:

- *Services connected with immovable property* are taxable in the country in which the property is situated. For example, an estate agent establishment in France selling a property situated in the UK is not taxable in France but, eventually, in the UK (if such an activity is not tax exempt in the UK).

- *Transport services* are taxable in the country in which the transport takes place, having regard to the distances covered. For example, where goods are transported from Italy into France, the French government will levy the tax on the part of the distance covered on French territory.

- *Some services are always taxed in the country in which they are physically carried out* regardless of the country in which the supplier is established. These include:

  — valuations of movable tangible property;
  — work on movable tangible property;
  — ancillary transport activities such as loading, unloading, handling and similar activities; and
  — cultural, artistic, sporting, scientific, educational, entertainment or similar activities, including the activities of the organisers of such activities.

  Consequently when such services are carried out in France they are taxable.

- *Intangible services:* Here the rules are somewhat more complex. The services concerned are the following:

  — hiring out of movable tangible property (with the exception of all forms of transport);
  — transfers and assignments of copyrights, patents, licences, trade marks and similar rights;
  — advertising services;
  — services of consultants, engineers, consultancy bureaux, lawyers, accountants and other similar services, as well as data processing and the supplying of information;
  — obligations to refrain from pursuing or exercising, in whole or in part, a business activity or a right referred to under this heading;

— banking, financial and insurance transactions including reinsurance, with the exception of the hire of safes;
— supply of staff;
— services of agents who act in the name of and for the account of another, when they procure for their principal the services referred to under this heading.

If the supplier and the customer are both established in France then French VAT applies. However, if the services are supplied from an entrepreneur established in France to a person not established in the EC, there is no taxation in France. The same applies where the services are supplied from an entrepreneur established in France to a *taxable* person established in another member state and the services are not taxable in France. But if the services are supplied by an entrepreneur established in France to a non-taxable customer established in another EC country then the tax is due in France.

Where services are supplied outside France to an entrepreneur established in France, VAT is due in France. Generally, the tax will be paid *by the client*. Where services are supplied into France from outside the EC to a non-taxpayer, the tax is due in France.

REGISTRATION

Any person who makes or expects to make taxable supplies in France upon which the tax due will exceed 1.350 FFr per year is required to register for VAT with the relevant tax authority.

France has not introduced the idea of a group into its VAT legislation; consequently all the transactions taking place between members of a group are normally subject to tax.

The following rules determine where an entrepreneur will be registered for VAT.

If there is a French place of business

The registration will be made at the principal French place of business and this address must be entered on the VAT registration form.

The VAT records and accounts should be kept and produced for inspection at that address. Someone at that address must be responsible for all VAT matters. If that person is an employee, he should normally be given written authority to act in this way.

If there is no French place of business

The entrepreneur may appoint an agent to act for him in VAT matters by letter of authority. Registration will then be made at the agent's address. The agent may be a company or a firm or an individual resident in France. Sufficient information must be given to the agent to enable him to keep VAT accounts, make returns and pay tax on the entrepreneur's behalf on a continuing basis. An agent appointed in this way must keep separate VAT accounts, and make separate VAT returns for his principal, in addition to those in respect of any VAT registration of his own. The remuneration paid to the agent is not subject to VAT.

IMPORTATION PROCEDURES

Misunderstanding of the French VAT importation procedures is a source of errors and the following guidelines provide a brief summary of the main principles:

If the place of supply is in France

If the entrepreneur is registered for VAT in France, he must be shown as the importer on the Customs entry. He will be allowed to reclaim the VAT paid on importation of the goods as input tax, subject to the normal rules. Any services supplied to the entrepreneur by an agent in arranging the supply will be standard-rated; this VAT may be reclaimed subject to the normal rules.

If the entrepreneur is not registered in France and supplies goods into France, the entrepreneur (seller) should normally pay VAT on importation, and on the selling price. The importation VAT can be offset.

Such an entrepreneur should use the services of a fiscal agent for the payment of the tax on the selling price. However, by concession, the need for foreign entrepreneurs to nominate a fiscal agent is eliminated if the goods imported do not need any processing between their importation and their delivery to the customers. The VAT on importation is then passed on for recovery to the customer, who receives the importation documents.

When the goods are sold into France through an agent, two situations can be envisaged, either:

- the agent takes part in the delivery of the goods in which case he then acts as if he is 'buying and reselling' the goods and pays VAT on importation unless the foreign entrepreneur is registered in France and pays VAT on delivery of the goods; or

- the agent does not take part in the delivery of the goods, in which case only the VAT on importation is due and this is passed on to the customer.

In both cases, the commission paid to the agent is exempt from VAT, since it must be included in the taxable value declared on importation. This contrasts with the position in the UK, for example, where, contrary to the Sixth Directive, VAT is due on the commission and may not be refundable.

If the place of supply is outside France

Normally, the customer will import the goods and pay the VAT on importation.

INPUT TAX DEDUCTION

Input tax is deductible, that is it can be set off insofar as it relates to an expense incurred for the needs of the business, used solely for the purpose of the business, or meant for the performance of taxable operations. The right to deduct is based on the possession of invoices showing the tax paid. Only the person to whom the supply is made is entitled to claim input tax deduction.

In France a distinction is made between capital assets and other expenses. So far as other expenses are concerned VAT is recoverable with a deferment of one calendar month. VAT incurred on certain limited expenses is not deductible. These include:

- goods and services used by the directors, personnel or others in respect of restaurants, entertainment and housing expenses and so on;
- cars;
- transportation of people;
- gifts;
- services relating to goods which are not deductible;
- certain products derived from petroleum; and
- prohibited advertisements.

When a taxable person has a number of different activities including both exempt and non-exempt items, the recovery of the input tax follows the following rules:

- for expenses solely used for taxable operations the VAT suffered is recoverable in total;
- for expenses used for exempt transactions the VAT is not recoverable; and
- for expenses used for both the tax is recoverable on a pro rata basis.

The amount by which any input tax exceeds the output tax may be refunded either at the end of the year in question or at the end of each calendar quarter.

ADMINISTRATION

VAT is administered by the Direction Generale des Impôts which also deals with the other taxes whether they are direct taxes or registration duties. The VAT on import is administered by the Customs authorities.

APPEALS

The taxable person may appeal against a decision made by the Direction Generale des Impôts. Appeals are made in writing to the administrative courts which are totally independent. After judgment by the administrative court a final appeal can be made to the Supreme Court (Conseil d'Etat).

VAT AND OTHER TAXES

A person who cannot recover input tax, for example because he makes only exempt supplies, can treat the irrecoverable VAT element as part of the cost for other tax purposes.

VAT REFUND PROCEDURES

Entrepreneurs resident in the European Community

1 **Can a claim for a refund be made by the entrepreneur direct to the French tax authorities?**
Yes. The claim may be made direct by the non-resident person or by his appointed agent.

2 **To what address should the claim be made?**
Centre des Impôts des non-residents
9 rue d'Uzes
75002 Paris.

3 **Which form should be submitted and in which language should it be completed?**
The claimant may use the French form VAT No 3559 which can be obtained from the address above or any of the standard forms used throughout the EC. Whichever version of the form is used it must be completed in French.

4 **What are the minimum amounts that may be reclaimed and how frequently can such claims be submitted?**
The general rules relating to time and cash limits are set out above. The minimum amounts which may be claimed from the French authorities are as follows:

	Minimum claim FFr
Calendar year claim	170
Intermediate claim (civil term)	1400

5 **What is the time limit for submitting a claim?**
The claim must be made before the expiry of the six months following the end of the relevant calendar year. In practice, the French authorities will not accept a claim which is received after the six month limit even if the postmark indicates that the claim was sent within the six month period.

6 **Is any French VAT not reclaimable?**
As explained in the introductory section, VAT cannot, in general, be reclaimed in respect of expenses incurred by an entrepreneur where his business would by its nature be treated as

exempt if it was carried on in the country of the claim. Nor can VAT be reimbursed on the purchase and rental of transport vehicles, catering, hotel accommodation, entertaining, petrol and expenses in relation to immovable property.

7   Which documents must be submitted with the repayment claim form?

A certificate of status, obtainable from the claimant's own tax authorities, proving that the claimant is registered for VAT in a member state, and the original invoices which will be stamped and returned, normally within one month.

8   How long, on average, will the authorities take to repay the amount claimed?

The authorities must make a refund within six months of receiving a satisfactory claim. In practice, claims are repaid well within this limit. If a claim is not satisfactory, delays will occur whilst enquiries are made of the claimant.

9   Is it necessary to appoint a fiscal representative in France and, if not, is it advisable to do so?

Claims may be made direct to the French tax authorities at the address above by the non-resident claimant or his non-resident appointed agent. Although there is no requirement to appoint a French agent to submit claims, an agent may well be able to assist in preparing proper claims and obtaining refunds as quickly as possible.

Entrepreneurs not resident in the European Community

10   Does the ability to make a claim also apply to non-EC entrepreneurs?

Currently, repayments of French VAT will be made only to entrepreneurs who sell goods to France, who supply exempted transport services and ancillary services or who supply services with respect to which the French recipient of the service is liable for VAT. These services are:

- sale and granting of copyrights;
- patents, trademarks, etc;
- advertising services;

- services rendered by consultants;
- data processing and supply of information;
- supply of staff; and
- letting of movable tangible property other than means of transport.

11 Is the procedure the same as for entrepreneurs resident in the EC?
No. The claim must be made through a French resident representative.

6 Federal Republic of Germany

SCOPE OF THE TAX

On 1 January 1968, the value-added tax (Mehrwertsteuer) replaced the cumulative all-stage turnover tax, which had been in effect for almost 50 years.

The Turnover Tax (VAT) Law of 1967 was amended and republished in 1973. It was revised with effect from 1 January 1980 in compliance with the EC Sixth Directive. Although the basic structure of the tax was not affected, the changes in detail were so numerous that few sections of the previous law remained untouched.

For VAT purposes the territory of Germany is the same as the Customs area of the country, which excludes the free ports and includes some segments of other countries that are subject to German Customs administration under international agreements. The City of West Berlin is part of the German Customs territory.

VAT is levied on taxable transactions carried out in Germany and West Berlin by an entrepreneur, regardless of whether the entrepreneur is a citizen or resident of Germany or has a place of management in the country.

Taxable transactions include:

- deliveries (mainly supplies of goods);
- other performances (mainly supplies of services);
- the withdrawal of business property for non-business purposes;
- application of business services to non-business purposes; and
- the importation of goods from abroad.

In order to become liable to the tax, there must be a consideration for the delivery or performance. VAT is generally assessed on the consideration.

Supplies of goods are the most important type of taxable supplies. These are defined as transactions by which an entrepreneur enables the customer acting on its own behalf to dispose of an object in its own name. The object of a delivery can be any type of tangible or intangible property, including energy which can be transferred, such as electricity and water, power, goodwill or an established clientele. The transfer of rights, however, is classified for VAT purposes as a service.

A service is anything that is not classified as a supply of goods. It can consist of an action or an omission or tolerating an act or a situation. Though there is an unlimited variety of possible taxable services the main cases are professional services, leases, licences, the sale of a patent or know-how, etc. A gratuitous performance is not subject to VAT. The law on this point is complex and care should be taken to ensure that supplies are correctly categorised.

Only transactions which take place in Germany are subject to VAT there and for VAT purposes it is important only that the individual performance is carried out in Germany and not that the entrepreneur is a citizen or resident of Germany or has its seat, place of management, or a permanent establishment there.

RATES OF TAX

VAT is chargeable at the standard rate of 14% and there is a reduced rate of 7%.

Principal supplies	*Rate*
Standard rate All supplies of goods and services except those taxable at 7% or those which are exempt.	14%
Reduced rate Food (but not when supplied in restaurants or hotels) Books and newspapers	7%

Passenger transport within a borough boundary or of less than 50 kilometres in distance

Exemptions

A sale or service is taxable unless specifically exempt. There is a long list of exemptions, covering mainly:

- exports and related supplies, including international transport;
- credit transactions and transfers of money or monetary debts and monetary options, securities, shares or other membership rights;
- supplies subject to other turnover or transfer taxes;
- medical and related supplies; and
- charitable supplies.

Importation is exempt only in rare situations. Outside the VAT Act itself, there are special exemptions for NATO forces, for US defence expenses and for other military-related matters.

The type of exemption is important for determining the entrepreneur's entitlement to recover fully the input tax billed to him by his suppliers. Export and related supplies are exempt with credit while for some financial transactions and property transactions it is possible to opt either to waive the tax exemption, in which case VAT must be charged and input tax can be recovered, or to claim the exemption and forfeit the credit.

To benefit from the exemption for exports and similar transactions, the taxpayer must meet particular documentation and bookkeeping requirements. There are substantive conditions for the exemption, not just a formality. The general rule is that the books and records must show:

- the consideration agreed or stipulated, with a breakdown between taxable transactions at different rates and exempt transactions;
- consideration received in part or in full for sales and other services not yet effected (with a similar break-down);
- the tax base for certain transactions with employees (in particular fringe benefits);
- the tax base for self-consumption and certain similar transactions with partners or shareholders;

- the consideration for taxable sales and other services supplied to the business for business purposes and the consideration paid in part or in full in advance and the VAT thereon;
- the tax base for the importation of items for the business and the VAT on importation.

A non-resident who is subject to these bookkeeping requirements does not have to keep the books within Germany but must make them available to the German authorities at any time if and when requested. They may be kept in any foreign language.

Preferential treatment for West Berlin

There are several reductions in VAT for West Berlin. These include:

- A special VAT reduction of between 2% and 10%, depending on the proportion of the value added in West Berlin to the gross turnover. This applies to:

  — deliveries of goods produced in West Berlin by a West Berlin entrepreneur for an entrepreneur in the Federal Republic and if the West Berlin entrepreneur has added value to his products. The West Berlin entrepreneur may reduce his VAT liability by a special percentage;

  — contracts for goods and services if a West Berlin entrepreneur produces an article with the help of material supplied by the customer or if he converts or improves such an article with his own material and the contract includes elements of both a sale and a contract of services;

  — rentals and leases of assets which are produced in West Berlin and rented or leased to an entrepreneur in the Federal Republic.

- A 6% reduction in the agreed rental of films, sound negatives and synchronisations for use in West Germany. For VAT purposes the reduction is the amount of consideration on which VAT is paid.

- A 10% deduction in the amount of consideration on which

VAT is due for certain advisory services of a commercial or technical nature together with, inter alia, the services of advertising agencies, etc the licensing of publication, film and theatrical rights, etc computer services, etc. To qualify the greater part of the services must be performed by an independent contractor in West Berlin.

Tax preferences in favour of the West German entrepreneur

The tax reduction which an entrepreneur in the Federal Republic can claim with respect to any one of the transactions listed above amounts to 4.2% of the agreed consideration.

TAX INVOICES

An entrepreneur who supplies goods or services has to issue a tax invoice which must include the following information:

- name and address of the supplier who makes the delivery or renders the service;
- name and address of the buyer of the goods or the recipient of the service;
- specification of the goods delivered or the type and volume of the services rendered;
- date of the delivery or other performance;
- consideration agreed; and
- amount of VAT due on the price of the goods sold or services rendered.

If the customer agrees, a less detailed invoice may be issued for supplies not exceeding DM 200.

PLACE OF SUPPLY

The distinction between supplies of goods and other services is important because of the different rules regarding the time and the place of supply.

Supplies of goods

In principle, a supply of goods is deemed to be made at the place where the object is located at the time that the right of disposal is obtained. If the entrepreneur transports the goods to the customer then the supply is deemed to be made when transportation starts and if he dispatches the goods to be supplied to a customer then the time of supply is the time of the hand-over to the dispatch agent.

A major exception to these rules is that delivery is deemed to be made in the country to which the import was made and import tax paid if the entrepreneur ships the goods from another member country of the EC and he or his agent is the taxpayer with respect to the import tax.

Performance of services

Regarding performance of services the basic rule is that these are carried out where the enterprise rendering the service is situated. But there are numerous exemptions from the basic rule, such as:

- *Services connected with real property* are considered to be rendered where the property is situated.

- *Transportation services* are deemed to be rendered where the act of transportation is carried out.

- *Some services are deemed to be supplied at the place where they are actually carried out.* These include artistic and educational services; entertainment; and improvements of property including servicing machines, vehicles or industrial installations.

- *Some services are deemed to be rendered at the place where the recipient's business is located.* These include advertising and publicity; legal, business or technical consultation services; electronic data processing; and procurement of personnel, etc.

REGISTRATION

Entrepreneurs who are *resident* in Germany and who make taxable supplies within Germany have to register for VAT at the local tax office (Finanzamt) and to file tax returns. In general, the taxable period for the computation and for the assessment is the calendar year. The annual return shows all supplies made during the year and all pre-tax and import taxes.

In addition, every entreprencur whose VAT liability for the preceding year exceeded DM 6,000 has to file monthly returns and pay the tax at the same time. If the tax liability did not exceed DM 6,000 for the prior year the entrepreneur has to pay VAT on a quarterly basis. Small entrepreneurs whose turnover plus tax during the preceding calendar year did not exceed DM 25,000 and whose turnover during the current calendar year is not expected to exceed DM 100,000, are exempt.

An entrepreneur who is *not resident* in Germany is not obliged to file tax returns, if he has only made supplies for which the customer or client is required to operate the withholding procedure.

The withholding procedure provides that where an entrepreneur who does not reside in Germany makes a taxable supply of services, then the recipient of the turnover transaction must withhold the VAT from the payment and pay it over to the tax office. If this withholding procedure does not apply, non-residents have to fulfil the same obligations concerning registration and tax returns as residents do.

VAT consolidation

Where two or more German resident companies are under common control they are to be registered as a single group for VAT purposes so that transactions between members of the VAT group are ignored and only one VAT return is rendered by the group.

IMPORTATION PROCEDURES

In Germany an import turnover tax (import tax) is levied on the importation of goods. The import tax is imposed on deliveries only and at the same tax rate which applies to taxable supplies of equivalent goods.

The import tax is usually payable together with the Customs duty. It is calculated on each individual import. The basis is the Customs value or the sales price of other imported goods. The tax is administered by the Customs authorities and it is governed by Customs law.

For the deduction of input tax, the import tax paid is treated in the same way as VAT on domestic purchases. For this reason the tax is not a cost factor since it is treated in the same way as regular domestic purchases.

INPUT TAX DEDUCTION

A domestic entrepreneur who files a tax return can deduct the following items as input tax when computing the VAT due:

- the tax invoiced separately by other entrepreneurs for supplies or other services which are carried out for his business;
- the import turnover tax paid on objects which have been imported into the territory of Germany for his business.

Subject to certain exemptions (mainly exports) the input tax may not be recovered for taxes on deliveries and services received which are:

- tax-exempt supplies;
- supplies outside Germany, which would be tax-exempt if they were executed within Germany;
- supplies and other services made free of charge, which would be tax-exempt if made for payment.

Thus, where an entrepreneur has both taxable and tax-exempt turnover transactions, the turnover tax charged to him and attributable to the tax-exempt turnover transactions is not recoverable.

The VAT charged to entrepreneurs who are not established in Germany and West Berlin may be refunded. The refund will be conditional on the taxable person having made no supply of goods or services to the fiscal territory during the refund period with the exception of:

- exempt transactions pursuant to UStG Section 4(3) such as the tax-exempt international carriage of goods and services connected with this; and

- transactions that have been subject to tax deduction (UStDV Sections 51 to 56) or individual taxation (UStG Section 16(5) and 18(5)).

ADMINISTRATION

VAT is administered by the Tax Authority which is responsible for collecting all taxes both direct and indirect and for conducting periodic tax audits. VAT records are always reviewed during a tax audit and in addition special VAT audits may be carried out from time to time. It is not therefore usually necessary to register separately for VAT purposes. In general, preliminary tax returns have to be filed on a monthly basis, the return and any payment being due on the tenth day of the following month.

APPEALS

A taxpayer may appeal against the tax authority's assessment within one month of receipt of the notice of the assessment. Appeals are dealt with by the local tax office in the first instance, but may then proceed to the Tax Court. An appeal against the decision of the Tax Court can, under certain conditions, be carried by either party to the Federal Court.

VAT AND OTHER TAXES

The entrepreneur who cannot recover input tax, for example because he only makes tax-exempt turnover transactions may treat the irrecoverable VAT element as part of the cost for other tax purposes. This also applies to those entrepreneurs who may only be entitled to partial VAT recovery due to partial exemption.

VAT REFUND PROCEDURES

Entrepreneurs resident in the European Community

1   **Can a claim for a refund be made by the entrepreneur direct to the German tax authorities?**
    Yes. The claim may be made by the non-resident entrepreneur.

2   **To what address should the claim be made?**
    The entrepreneur should apply for refund to the Federal Finance Office as follows:

    Bundesamt für Finanzen
    Friedhofstrasse 1
    5300 Bonn 3.

    At the request of the taxable person, any tax office in Germany and West Berlin may deal with a claim.

3   **Which form should be submitted and in which language should it be completed?**
    The claimant may use the German form USt 1T (Application for refund of VAT) obtainable from the above address or any of the standard forms used throughout the EC. Whichever version of the form is used, it must be completed in German.

4   **What are the minimum amounts that may be reclaimed and how frequently can such claims be submitted?**
    The general rules relating to time and cash limits are set out in the introduction. The minimum amounts which may be claimed from the German authorities are as follows:

	Minimum claim DM
Calendar year claim	60
Intermediate claim	500
Claim for remainder of calendar year	60

The taxable person may, at his option, apply for a refund for a period (refund period) of not less than three consecutive months in one calendar year. The refund period may not exceed one calendar year. The application should relate to all amounts of value added tax falling within the refund period. The refund period may be less than three months where it represents the remainder of the calendar year. In the application relating to this period the taxable person may include claims which relate to preceding refund periods in the calendar year concerned, where such claims have not been made in previous applications.

5   What is the time limit for submitting a claim?
The application for refund must be received by the competent authority not later than 30 June of the year following the year in which the tax was incurred. In certain cases an extension of time is possible. The application should be typed or completed in block letters.

6   Is any German VAT not reclaimable?
The input tax must originate in the business of the non-resident entrepreneur. VAT charged to a non-resident entrepreneur and related to transactions outside the fiscal territory which, if effected by the entrepreneur within that territory would preclude the decuction of input tax, cannot be reclaimed.

7   Which documents must be submitted with the repayment claim form?
The application must be accompanied by a certificate issued by the state in which the taxable person is established, showing that the claimant is registered as a taxable person in that state. This certificate will be valid for one year from the date of issue. The application must also be accompanied by the originals of the invoices and import documents. The total amount of tax refund must be calculated by the taxable person.

8   How long, on average, will the authorities take to repay the amount claimed?
Repayment of the amount charged will take about two to three months.

9   Is it necessary to appoint a fiscal representative in Germany and, if not, is it advisable to do so?
Claims may be made direct to the tax authorities at the address above by either the non-resident claimant or his appointed agent. Although there is no requirement to appoint an agent

to submit claims, an agent may well be able to assist in preparing proper claims and obtaining refunds as quickly as possible.

Entrepreneurs not resident in the European Community

10 Does the ability to make a claim also apply to non-EC entrepreneurs?
Yes. A refund of input tax may also be made to entrepreneurs outside the EC.

11 Is the procedure the same as for entrepreneurs resident in the EC?
Yes. The procedure is the same for entrepreneurs resident outside the EC as for those resident within the EC.

7 Greece

SCOPE OF THE TAX

Value Added Tax (Foros Prostithemenis Axia (FPA)) was introduced on 1 January 1987 to replace a dozen or so indirect taxes such
as tax on turnover and stamp duties. The legislation was adapted in
accordance with the EC Sixth, Eighth and Tenth Directives.

VAT is implemented within the national territory of Greece with
the exception of Mount Athos (Agion Oris).

VAT is charged on:

- any supply of goods or services made in Greece which is a
  taxable supply, made by a 'taxable person', in the course or
  furtherance of a 'business'; and
- the importation of goods into Greece by any person (not only
  a 'taxable person').

Small enterprises are exempt from all obligations concerning
VAT if the annual turnover is less than GrD 1,000,000 for the
supply of goods or GrD 250,000 for the supply of services.

RATES OF TAX

The current standard rate of VAT is 18% with a reduced rate of 6%
and an increased rate of 36%.

For the Dodekanissa region the reduced and standard rates are
decreased by 30%. This gives a reduced rate of 4% and a standard
rate of 11%. The increased rate is reduced by 15% to 31%. These
special lower rates apply on the supply of goods by a taxable person
who is established in this region and also on imported goods in the

region. The supply or importation of tobacco products, petroluem products and electricity and also the supply of services are taxable at the normal rates of 6%, 18% and 36%.

Principal supplies	*Rate*
Reduced rate	6%

(Annex II of the Law)
Goods for gross consumption including food, drugs and medicines, ordinary wines, cars (with some exemptions) and paper, books, newspapers and reviews.

(There is a 50% deduction on the 6% VAT for the following items which makes them taxable at a rate of 3%.)

Transportation of people and merchandise, hotel accommodation, services rendered by liberal professionals (except doctors, lawyers, notaries, and so on), agricultural services and advertising.	3%

Standard rate	18%

All supplies of goods and services in Greece except those which are specifically taxable at the other two rates or exempt.

Increased rate	36%

Luxury goods and services including perfumes, jewellery, tobacco products, alcoholic beverages (rum, gin, whisky, vodka, tequila, arak and taffia), colour television sets, furs, clocks and watches, entertainment and services in the luxury class and bars of any category.

Certain operations although falling within the scope of VAT are exempt because of particular stipulations in the law. The main types of *exempt* supplies are:

- certain land transactions;
- insurance;
- financial transactions;

- education, health, sport and competition;
- postal services;
- radio and television services;
- water supply (not bottled).

Exports are exempt with credit.

TAX INVOICES

When a registered person supplies goods or services to another, he must issue an invoice stamped by the Tax Service. The recipient must retain this in order to reclaim input tax. Tax invoices must show:

- serial number;
- tax point;
- supplier's name and address;
- customer's name and address;
- type of supply;
- rate of tax; and
- total tax chargeable.

For retail sales special receipts are issued which include the tax in the price.

PLACE OF SUPPLY

The distinction between whether a supply is one of goods or one of services is important because the rules governing the time and place of supply are different and, on occasions, it may decide whether the supply is taxable or not.

Supplies of goods

The place of supply of goods depends on where the goods are when they are allocated or designated to a specific order from a customer. A supply takes place in Greece if the specific goods to be supplied are located in Greece. This applies even if the supplier has no place of business in Greece or intends to export the goods to somewhere outside Greece. For example, a US company may purchase goods located in Greece for sale to another Greek person or for export and VAT will be due but may be refunded when the goods are exported.

However, if the contract requires the supplier to process the goods in Greece before the buyer takes property in the goods, the supply is still made in Greece. This is because a supply of processed goods is being made. The importation of the goods is a necessary preliminary step before the supply is made. The scheme also applies to the assembly of goods when this takes place in Greece.

Supplies of services

As a general rule, a supply of services is treated as taking place in Greece if the supplier 'is established' in Greece. An entrepreneur is established in Greece if he has a business or some other fixed establishment in Greece. There are some exceptions to the general rule and some services are taxable in Greece according to the following criteria:

- Location of real property.
  According to the above criterion, certain services related to the building such as architects, engineers and real estate agents services are taxed in Greece.

- Place of implementation of the service.
  This criterion is applied to the following services:

  — transport and closely related services (loading, unloading, etc);
  — installation or assembly services in connection with imported goods when the supplier is established abroad;
  — cultural, artistic, athletic, scientific, educational, entertainment or similar activities;
  — expertise and work closely related to tangible goods.

- Place where the goods are used.
  This applies to the leasing of means of transport. The supply of services is taxed in Greece when the lessor is established in Greece and the lessee uses the transport in the interior of the country or in another EC country or where the lessor is established outside the EC and the lessee uses the means of transport in Greek territory.

- Intangible services.

  Some services are considered to take place in Greece and consequently they are taxable there when they are supplied either by persons established in another EC country to a recipient (taxable person) established in Greece, or by persons who are established in a third (non-EC) country to any recipient (taxable person or not) established in Greece. The services covered are:

  — the assignment/transfer of copyrights, patents, licences, trademarks and similar rights;
  — advertising services;
  — services of consultants, engineers, consultancy bureaux, lawyers and accountants;
  — the supply of staff;
  — insurance, financial and banking services with the exemption of the hire of safes; and
  — the hiring out of tangible movable property with the exception of all forms of transport.

REGISTRATION

All taxable persons (those who have an annual turnover of more than GrD 1,000,000 for the supply of goods or GrD 250,000 for the supply of services) are required to notify the Tax Authorities of the commencement, change or suspension of their operations as well as any change in their firm or the location of the establishment. On notification a tax registration number is acquired. In addition, registered traders are required to issue documents according to the tax regulations such as invoices, retail receipts etc and to keep in a special file all documents which include any information concerning VAT deductions and liabilities.

Taxable persons who are not located in Greece but make taxable transactions there, are required to appoint an authorised tax representative with permanent residence in Greece.

Any entrepreneurs who are not established in Greece and who do not have any taxable operations there can reclaim the VAT input tax for goods and services under the EC Eighth Directive.

IMPORTATION PROCEDURES

The importation procedures follow the Sixth Directive and the Customs Rules and VAT becomes chargeable when the goods are cleared through Customs for consumption or disposal.

INPUT TAX DEDUCTION

According to the normal rules, every taxable person may deduct the input tax in respect of taxable (business) operations. If a taxable person makes both taxable and exempt supplies the input tax incurred must be apportioned to compute the recoverable amount of input tax attributable to the taxable supplies.

VAT incurred on the following goods or services is not deductible at all:

- importation or acquisition of private cars for up to nine passengers; motorcycles; ships and aircraft to be used for recreational purposes. Also the related expenses for fuel, repairs, maintenance, leasing and any other similar expenses of the above;
- expenses of receptions, hospitality and entertainment in general;
- imports or purchase of manufactured tobacco;
- imports or purchase of alcoholic beverages if they are used in respect of exempt operations.

ADMINISTRATION

VAT is administered on importation by Customs and by the tax authorities as for any other tax on taxable operations within Greece. Automatic, and in some cases severe, financial and penal punishments have been introduced into the Greek VAT system particularly by the laws which regulate the keeping of records and the issue of invoices and receipts.

APPEALS

A person may appeal against a decision by the tax authority according to the law of tax procedure. Appeals are heard by independent Administrative Tax Tribunals in the first and second instance. Also they may proceed, on a point of law only, to the Council of the State.

VAT AND OTHER TAXES

A person who cannot recover input tax, for example because he makes only exempt supplies, can treat the irrecoverable VAT elements as part of the cost for other tax purposes (income taxation). This applies also to those registered persons who may only be entitled to partial VAT recovery due to partial exemption.

VAT REFUND PROCEDURES

Entrepreneurs resident in the European Community

1 **Can a claim for a refund be made by the entrepreneur direct
   to the Greek VAT authorities?**
   Yes. The claim may be made direct by the non-resident person
   or his appointed agent. The appointment of an agent is obliga-
   tory when two or more taxable persons are named on the
   invoice or import document. The claim may be sent by registered letter addressed to the Greek VAT authorities.

2 **To what address should the claim be made?**
   Diefthinsi Meleton ke forun FPA Ipourgiou Iconomikon
   2–4 Sina Str 106–72
   Athens
   (Ministry of Finance VAT Directorate of Studies and Own
   Resources, 2–4 Sina Str 106–72, Athens.)

3 **Which form should be submitted and in which language
   should it be completed?**
   The claimant must use the special model – form A – obtainable
   from the address above. This form must be completed in Greek.

4 **What are the minimum amounts that may be reclaimed and
   how frequently can such claims be submitted?**
   The general rules relating to time and cash limits are set out in
   the introduction. The minimum amounts that may be claimed
   from Greek authorities are as follows:

   | | Minimum claim |
	GrD
Calendar year claim	3,750
Intermediate claim	30,000
Claim for remainder of calendar year	3,750

5 **What is the time limit for submitting a claim?**
   The claim must be made before the expiry of the six months following the end of the relevant calendar year. In practice, the Greek
   Authorities will accept a claim which is received after the six
   month limit provided that the postmark (of the registered letter)
   indicates that the claim was sent within the six month period.

6   Is any Greek VAT not reclaimable?

Greek VAT cannot be reclaimed in the following cases:

- supply of goods and services which do not give right of deduction of the tax (purchase of new cars, entertainment expenses, etc);
- supply of goods and services which are not related to the economic activities of the taxable persons;
- expenses incurred by an entrepreneur where his business would by its nature be treated as exempt if he was carrying it on in the country of the claim; or
- where the special schemes for small undertakings, farmers or tour operators set out in the Sixth Directive are used.

7   Which documents must be submitted with the repayment claim form?

The following documents must be submitted with the repayment form:

- a certificate of status, obtainable from the claimant's own Tax Authorities, providing that the claimant is registered for VAT in a member state. This must be translated into the Greek language. This certificate is in force for one year, but a new form is not required where another claim is submitted in the same year unless the status of the claimant has changed;
- the original invoices, or the other document serving as the original invoice, or the Customs document in the case of imports. These documents will be stamped and returned, normally within one month;
- an official declaration by the claimant that he had made a taxable supply of goods or services into Greece, with the exception of the services provided for by the Greek VAT Law (L 1642 art 12 para 3). This declaration is incorporated in the text of form A (see question 3 above).

8   How long, on average, will the authorities take to repay the amount claimed?

The authorities must refund the amount claimed within six months of receiving a satisfactory claim. In practice, claims are repaid well within this limit. If a claim is not satisfactorily proven, delays will occur whilst enquiries on the claimant are made.

9   Is it necessary to appoint a fiscal representative in Greece and, if not, is it advisable to do so?
Claims may be made direct to the Greek authorities at the address above by the non-resident claimant or his non-resident appointed agent. Although there is no requirement to appoint a Greek agent to submit claims, an agent may well be able to assist in preparing proper claims and carrying out all necessary proceedings for obtaining refunds as quickly as possible.

Entrepreneurs not resident in the European Community

10   Does the ability to make a claim also apply to non-EC entrepreneurs?
An entrepreneur registered for business purposes in a non-EC country can use the scheme to reclaim VAT paid in Greece in the same way as EC claimants provided that the additional provision of reciprocity is met. This provision means that the non-EC country should offer a reciprocal right of refund of VAT or any other domestic turnover or consumption tax levied to Greek entrepreneurs.

11   Is the procedure the same as for entrepreneurs resident in the EC?
Yes. The procedure is the same; the only problem is the practical meaning of the term 'reciprocity' which has yet to be defined.

8 Republic of Ireland

SCOPE OF THE TAX

The Value Added Tax Act 1972 brought VAT into operation on 1 November 1972. Subsequently, major changes were made in the annual Financial Acts and the Value Added Tax Amendment Act 1978.

For VAT purposes Ireland comprises the Republic of Ireland excluding Northern Ireland.

VAT is charged when a taxable person supplies, that is sells or provides, taxable goods or services within Ireland in the course or furtherance of business. It is also charged on the importation of goods and certain services into Ireland at the same rates applicable to taxable supplies within the country.

Business transactions in Ireland are generally liable to VAT and are called 'taxable supplies'. A person who makes taxable supplies of goods above IR£32,000 per annum, or taxable supplies of services above IR£15,000 per annum is obliged to register for VAT.

RATES OF TAX

The standard rate of VAT is 23%.

Principal supplies	*Rate*
Special reduced rate	5%
Electricity.	
Reduced rate	10%
Coal, gas, peat, concrete, building and agricultural	

services, car repairs, newspapers, clothing and
footwear except children's, hotel accommodation,
meals, takeaway hot food, car boat and caravan hire,
hairdressing, laundry and cleaning, repairs to electrical
goods, cinema, driving instruction, photographic and
tour guide services, waste disposal.

Standard rate   23%
Goods and services not liable at lower rates.

The main types of *zero-rated* supplies are as follows:

- exports;
- food;
- electricity;
- children's footwear and clothing;
- medicines; and
- medical equipment and appliances.

The main types of *exempt* supplies are as follows:

- medical, dental, and veterinary supplies;
- education;
- short leases;
- transport;
- banking, insurance, stockbrokers;
- theatres;
- sporting events, sporting facilities, lotteries, bloodstock and
  greyhounds;
- funeral undertakers; and
- certain agency services such as travel.

TAX INVOICES

When a registered person supplies goods or services to another he
must issue a tax invoice. The recipient must retain this in order to
reclaim input tax. The invoices must show:

- name and address of the person issuing the invoice;
- his VAT number;
- name and address of customer;
- date of issue of invoice;

- date of supply of goods or services;
- full description of the goods or services;
- amount charged including VAT;
- rate including zero-rate; and
- amount of VAT at each rate.

A VAT invoice need not be issued in respect of supplies to unregistered persons except unregistered persons entitled to repayment such as foreign traders.

PLACE OF SUPPLY

The distinction between whether a supply is one of goods or one of services is important because the rate of tax may depend on which it is and also the rules governing the time and place of supply are different for services and for goods.

Supplies of goods

The place of supply of goods depends on where the goods are when they are allocated or designated to a specific order from a customer. A supply takes place in Ireland if the specific goods to be supplied are located in Ireland. This applies even if the supplier has no place of business in Ireland or intends to export the goods to somewhere outside Ireland. If the goods are outside Ireland at the time they are allocated to a specific order, the supply takes place outside Ireland even if the supplier has a place of business within Ireland. Any work such as processing, adapting or installing goods in Ireland means that the place of supply is Ireland.

Supplies of services

Supplies of services are made in Ireland if the supplier is Irish based. A business is Irish based if it has a business or some other fixed establishment in Ireland eg office, showroom, factory, mobile workshop or building site. A business carried on through a branch or agency is also a fixed establishment and liable to account for Irish VAT on supplies of services. If the entrepreneur has business establishments in more than one country and supplies services, the common rules adopted by EC member states will determine that VAT is chargeable on services supplied in the state where the property is located in relation to which the services are made.

REGISTRATION

Persons who make taxable supplies of services of more than IR£15,000 per year or taxable supplies of goods of more than IR£22,000 per year are obliged to register for VAT.

Groups of companies under common control may be treated as a single taxable entity so that transfers between members of the group do not give rise to any VAT. Because it may take some time to assemble the information for the VAT Return there is a concession to allow the transactions reflected in the VAT Return to be those of one month earlier than the particular VAT period.

The following rules determine where an entrepreneur will be registered for VAT:

- If there is an Irish place of business.
  The registration will be made at the principal Irish place of business and this address is to be entered on the VAT Registration Form. The VAT records and accounts should be kept and produced for inspection at that address.

- If there is no Irish place of business.
  The registration will be made at an agent's address within the state and this address is to be entered on the VAT Registration Form. The records should be available for inspection when requested at the agent's address but there is no requirement to keep the records within the state.

IMPORTATION PROCEDURES

- If the place of supply is in Ireland.
  If the entrepreneur is registered for VAT in Ireland he should be shown as the importer on the Customs documentation. He will be allowed to reclaim the VAT paid or deferred on importation of the goods as input tax subject to the normal rules.

- If the place of supply is outside Ireland.
  Normally the customer will import the goods and pay or defer the VAT on importation. Alternatively, if arrangements exist for the importer to pay the VAT on behalf of the supplier only the named customer can treat the VAT paid at importation as input tax.

INPUT TAX DEDUCTION

Possession of a tax invoice or a stamped copy of the Customs entry is essential to substantiate a claim to deduct input tax such as VAT incurred on raw materials. Only the person to whom the supply is made is entitled to claim input tax deduction and this may not necessarily be the person who pays for the supply. If goods are used only partly for business purposes only VAT on the proportion attributable to business use may be claimed. No deduction is allowed for VAT incurred on passenger motor vehicles, petrol, entertainment expenses and the provision of food, drink and accommodation.

A registered person who makes only taxable supplies is not restricted as to the amount of deductible input tax he may claim apart from the items mentioned above. A person who makes only exempt supplies, however, is not entitled to register at all and cannot therefore claim any VAT as input tax. A person making both taxable and exempt supplies may be entitled only to a proportion of his input tax pro rata to his chargeable sales.

Registered persons are entitled to claim in their VAT returns a credit equal to 2.0% of the amount excluding VAT paid to unregistered farmers for agricultural products and services. This is being increased to 2.3% from 1 March 1990.

ADMINISTRATION

VAT is administered by the Revenue Commissioners who are responsible to the Minister for Finance. VAT at local level is administered by the Inspector of Taxes dealing with the income of companies and individuals in that area. Computerised summaries of VAT returns are cross-checked with the information for income tax and corporation tax. VAT on imports is administered at local level by the Customs and Excise Division of the Revenue Commissioners. VAT returns are issued by and returned to the Collector General's office. This office deals with all queries in relation to the payment and repayment of VAT by registered persons. The Collector General's office is also entitled to raise estimated assessments when no returns are submitted.

Taxable persons must make returns and payment of VAT between the 10th and 19th days following the end of a taxable period. Each taxable period is a period of two months, beginning on the 1st day of January, March, May, July, September and November (ie six taxable periods each year).

Annual accounting for VAT

This is a new feature of VAT administration in Ireland. The Collector-General is empowered to authorise taxable persons to submit a return and pay the tax outstanding in respect of a number (not exceeding six) of consecutive taxable periods. The Collector-General may take account of certain circumstances (eg suitability or otherwise of a case for the procedure), to impose certain conditions when issuing an authorisation (such as the making of payments on account) and to terminate an authorisation.

APPEALS

As with other taxes, decisions by the Revenue Commissioners on VAT matters are subject to a right of appeal to the Tax Appeal Commissioners and subsequently to the Circuit Court. Points of law may be appealed to the High Court and finally the Supreme Court.

VAT AND OTHER TAXES

Persons who are not registered because their sales are below the registration limit or their activity is exempt can treat the irrecoverable VAT element as part of the cost for other tax purposes.

VAT REFUND PROCEDURES

Entrepreneurs resident in the European Community

1   **Can a claim for a refund be made by the entrepreneur direct to the Irish VAT authorities?**
Yes. A non-resident person can claim direct.

2   **To what address should the claim be made?**
Revenue Commissioners
VAT Repayments Section
Castle House
South Great Georges Street
Dublin 2.

3   **Which form should be submitted and in which language should it be completed?**
Irish Form VAT 60 completed in English.

4   **What are the minimum amounts that may be reclaimed and how frequently can such claims be submitted?**
The general rules relating to time and cash limits are set out in the introduction. The minimum amounts which may be claimed from the Irish authorities are as follows:

	Minimum claim
	IR
Calendar year claim	16
Intermediate claim	130
Claim for remainder of calendar year	16

Claims can be submitted for a minimum period of three months and maximum of one year. An application may also be made to have services supplied without a charge to VAT where they are effected on a regular and continuing basis.

5   **What is the time limit for submitting a claim?**
The claim should be made within six months of the end of the calendar year but in practice no claim is refused.

6   **Is any Irish VAT not reclaimable?**
VAT incurred by exempt businesses and VAT on food and drink, hotel accommodation, personal services, entertainment

expenses, motor cars, petrol and goods and services used for non-business purposes are not reclaimable.

7 Which documents must be submitted with the repayment claim form?
Certificate of status (issued by the entrepreneur's own tax authorities), the original invoices and Customs documents.

8 How long, on average, will the authorities take to repay the amount claimed?
Normally six weeks but the claim must be repaid within six months.

9 Is it necessary to appoint a fiscal representative in Ireland and, if not, is it advisable to do so?
This is not necessary but it does speed the matter up as the relevant offices of the Revenue Commissioners are under-staffed.

Entrepreneurs not resident in the European Community

10 Does the ability to make a claim also apply to non-EC entrepreneurs?
Yes. Non-EC entrepreneurs can reclaim Irish VAT.

11 Is the procedure the same as for entrepreneurs resident in the EC?
The procedure is similar but documentary evidence of involvement in a trading activity must be submitted instead of a Certificate of Status.

9 Italy

SCOPE OF THE TAX

Imposta sul Valore Aggiunto (IVA) was introduced in Italy to replace Imposta Generale sull'Entrata (IGE) with effect from 1 January 1973. The legislation has been amended several times.

For VAT purposes Italy comprises the territory subject to the sovereignty of the Italian Republic, except for the three border areas of Livigno, Campione d'Italia and Lugano lake waters, which are not subject to VAT.

VAT is charged on:

- the supply of goods or services made in Italy by enterprises, artists or professionals; and
- the importation of goods into Italy by any person.

An entrepreneur is an individual carrying on a business activity on a continuing basis, even though such activity is not the sole or the main activity carried on by the entrepreneur. Companies and business partnerships are always deemed to be entrepreneurs. Similarly, artists and professional persons or partnerships are considered to be taxable persons for VAT purposes if their activity is carried out on a continuing basis.

For VAT purposes, transfers of goods are basically defined as sales of goods. However, some other transactions are deemed to be taxable transfers, for example the free transfer of goods usually produced or dealt in by a firm, while certain sales are deemed not to be taxable transfers, for example the sale of a firm. In a similar way, certain transactions are specifically deemed to be taxable performances of services, such as the lease of goods, while some others are deemed not to be taxable, such as the assignment of rights, licences and copyrights on works produced by the author or his heirs.

RATES OF TAX

The current standard rate of VAT is 19%.

Principal supplies	*Rate*
Special reduced rate	4%
Farming and fishing products and other products specifically listed.	
Normal reduced rate	9%
Food, clothing, records, tapes, oil and fuel products and other products specifically listed.	
Standard rate	19%
Increased rate	38%
Furs, certain cars and motorcycles, certain pleasure craft and other luxury items.	

Furthermore, certain listed transactions are *exempt* from VAT. These include:

• insurance;
• most financial operations; and
• medicine, etc.

VAT is not charged on export transactions.

It is compulsory to issue invoices for exempt and export transactions as well as for taxable transactions.

TAX INVOICES

For each taxable transaction, as well as for certain non-taxable transactions, the supplier of goods or services must issue a tax invoice showing, among other things:

• supplier's name and address and VAT code number;

- customer's name and address;
- a date;
- a serial number;
- details of quality and quantity of goods or services supplied;
- prices;
- rates of tax; and
- total tax chargeable.

The information on the invoice must be recorded by the supplier in his own register of invoices issued. A copy of the invoice must be given to the customer, who records it in his register of invoices received.

Retailers are not required to issue invoices unless this is requested by the customer, but they have to record each transaction by means of an approved electronic sales register.

PLACE OF SUPPLY

Supplies of goods

The supply of goods is deemed to be made in Italy if such goods are physically within the Italian territory as defined above. This applies even if the supplier has no place of business in Italy. Alternatively, if the goods are outside Italy at the time that they are allocated to a specific order, the supply takes place outside Italy even if the supplier has a place of business within Italy.

However, a supply does not take place in Italy (but invoicing is required) when:

- the supplier exports the goods directly;
- the customer exports the goods within 90 days from the supply; or
- the customer qualifies as a 'usual exporter', that is one who exported goods at a value in excess of 10% of his turnover in the previous year.

The following supplies are also deemed not to take place in Italy:

- supply of ships for commercial use or fishing or sea rescue;
- supply of ships and aircraft and satellites to the Italian State; and

- supply of engines, spare parts and ships' stores for the ships and aircraft indicated above.

Supplies of services

A supply of services is deemed to take place in Italy if the supplier is domiciled or resident in Italy or if it is a permanent establishment in Italy of a person or legal entity domiciled and resident abroad. The domicile of partnerships, companies and other legal entities is their registered office, while the residence is where their effective management is situated.

A supply of services is treated as taking place in Italy if the supplier is a permanent establishment abroad of an entrepreneur domiciled or resident in Italy.

For certain services the distinction between whether a supply is made in Italy or not depends on specific rules.

- Goods or services transferred between different parts of a single legal entity are normally disregarded for the purposes of Italian VAT, except in the case of a sale of goods or services made by an Italian company or branch to its foreign branch/company and vice versa.

- Transport services are taxable in the country where the transport effectively takes place in proportion to the distances covered. For example, where goods are transported from France into Italy the Italian government will levy tax on the part of the journey covered on Italian territory.

REGISTRATION

Persons who make supplies of goods or business or professional services in Italy on a continuing basis are required to register for VAT with the competent VAT office *within 30 days from the start of their activity*. There is no minimum turnover exemption for VAT registration purposes. The Ministry of Finance is very strict regarding whether supplies are made on a continuing basis rather than on an occasional basis.

Every year, all VAT taxpayers must file the annual VAT return by

5 March reporting VAT transactions by reference to the previous calendar year.

A company which owns an interest of more than 50% of the voting shares in another company or companies can consolidate VAT payments starting from the second calendar year after that in which the required interest is acquired.

The following rules determine where a person or legal entity will be registered for VAT.

If there is an Italian place of business

The registration will be made with the VAT office competent for the registered office or permanent establishment of the person or legal entity by filing the appropriate VAT registration form. The VAT records and accounts should be kept and produced for inspection at the address indicated on the registration form.

If there is no Italian place of business

Non-resident persons or legal entities which do not have a permanent establishment in Italy are not required to register with the VAT office.

All the legal requirements such as invoicing and paying VAT to the Tax Office which derive from VAT supplies made or received by non-resident persons or legal entities without a permanent establishment in Italy may be complied with by a properly appointed Italian representative. Registration will then be made at the representative's address.

A representative appointed in this way must keep separate VAT accounts and make separate VAT returns for his principal, in addition to those in respect of any VAT registration of his own. In the case of violations of the VAT requirements, the representative is personally liable for penalties, together with his principal.

Where services are provided by non-residents, if no Italian representative is appointed the Italian customer must issue the invoices and calculate the VAT due which he can then credit against his tax liability in the normal way so that no charge will result.

IMPORTATION PROCEDURES

VAT is charged by and must be paid directly to Customs when the goods are imported into Italy. Customs then issues a bill which gives title to the customer for deduction as input tax.

No VAT is charged on import of exempt or non-taxable goods and on import of goods by 'usual exporters'. Proper documentation must be produced to the Customs in order to benefit from these exemptions.

INPUT TAX DEDUCTION

VAT charged to customers has to be paid monthly to the competent VAT office (or on a quarterly basis if total taxable supplies do not exceed Lir360 million a year in value), after deducting VAT incurred on purchases relating to business or professional activity.

Where some of the transactions effected are exempt from VAT, the amount of deductible VAT on purchases is proportionally reduced.

VAT at the increased rate of 38% is not deductible, unless the activity relates to the trade or manufacturing of such goods. The same applies for VAT charged by hotels and restaurants and for other purchases specifically indicated by the law, including the purchase of new or used cars and costs thereon.

ADMINISTRATION

The Ministry of Finance has overall charge of the application, regulation and collection of VAT in Italy through the VAT offices which are located in each Italian Province.

In the case of violations of the VAT law, severe financial – and sometimes criminal – penalties are imposed.

APPEALS

A person or legal entity may appeal against a decision by a VAT office. Appeals are heard by independent tax tribunals in the first and second instances but may then proceed, on a point of law only, to the Central Tax Commission (or the Court of Appeal) and the Supreme Court.

VAT AND OTHER TAXES

If the deduction of VAT on purchases is not allowed, then the VAT charged represents a cost for income tax purposes.

VAT REFUND PROCEDURES

Entrepreneurs resident in the European Community

1 **Can a claim for a refund be made by the entrepreneur direct to the Italian tax authorities?**
   Yes. The claim may be made directly by the non-resident person or his duly appointed agent.

2 **To what address should the claim be made?**
   Ufficio Provinciale dell'Imposta sul Valore Aggiunto
   viale Tolstoi 5
   00144 Roma.

3 **Which form should be submitted and in which language should it be completed?**
   The claimant may use the Italian form Mod IVA F TASSE 553 or any of the standard forms used throughout the EC. Whichever version of the form is used it must be completed in block capital letters in Italian.

4 **What are the minimum amounts that may be reclaimed and how frequently can such claims be submitted?**
   The general rules relating to time and cash limits are set out in the introduction. The minimum amounts which may be claimed from the Italian authorities are as follows:

	Minimum claim Lira
Calendar year claim	38,000
Intermediate claim	304,000
Claim for remainder of calendar year	38,000

5 **What is the time limit for submitting a claim?**
   The claim must be filed by the end of the sixth month following the end of the relevant calendar year. If the claim is sent by registered letter, the date of claim is that indicated by the postmark.

6 **Is any Italian VAT not reclaimable?**
   Non-deductible VAT (see above) cannot be reclaimed.

7 **Which documents must be submitted with the repayment claim form?**

The repayment claim form must be submitted with the following documents:

- original invoices, which must be written in Italian or in two or more languages, one of which must be Italian, unless they are translated into Italian with a notarised translation; and
- a certificate of status, obtainable from the claimant's tax authorities, proving that the claimant is registered for VAT in a member state; this certificate is valid for one year from its date of issue.

8   How long, on average, will the authorities take to repay the amount claimed?
Normally VAT is not refunded less than two years from the filing date. As internal procedures are not very well defined the VAT authorities often require more information and further delays are suffered.

9   Is it necessary to appoint a fiscal representative in Italy and, if not, is it advisable to do so?
Although there is no requirement to appoint an Italian fiscal representative, it is highly advisable to do so in order to obtain assistance in preparing claims and obtaining refunds as quickly as possible.

Entrepreneurs not resident in the European Community

10   Does the ability to make a claim also apply to non-EC entrepreneurs?
Non-EC entrepreneurs can claim only VAT incurred in Italy taking part in trade fairs, exhibitions and so on. Non-EC entrepreneurs carrying on a transport activity can also claim VAT incurred in Italy relating to such activity.

11   Is the procedure the same as for entrepreneurs resident in the EC?
Yes, the procedure is the same as for entrepreneurs resident in the EC.

10 Luxembourg

SCOPE OF THE TAX

The relevant VAT regulations are based on the law of 5 August 1969 as modified by the law of 12 February 1979 in connection with the Grand-Duchy's resolution of 23 May 1980 executing article 55 and section 2 and various other resolutions.

VAT is charged on:

- any supply of goods or services in Luxembourg which is a taxable supply made by a taxable person in the course or furtherance of a business for a valuable consideration;
- the importation of goods into Luxembourg by any person (not only a taxable person); and
- self-supplies in the course or furtherance of a business.

The 'supply of goods' is defined as the transfer of the power of disposal.

The power of disposal is, for these purposes, merely defined in economic terms to include for example the sale of stolen goods. Furthermore, various other acts are deemed to be the supply of goods; expropriation, commission marketing, sale of consigned goods, delivery on completion of a contract to manufacture for example. Other acts are deemed not to be a supply of goods.

VAT is also charged on the supply of services as well. This term is broadly defined as 'supply of anything other than goods'. Even though encompassing a large number of transactions, certain transactions are deemed not to be supplies of services. Supplies containing both elements are deemed in law to be supplies of either goods or services depending on which element is the greater.

A 'taxable person' is any person (individual, partnership, company, trustee, club, association, charity, etc) who has to be registered for VAT. A person is not obliged to register if his taxable supplies do not exceed in value the annual turnover of Lfrs 200,000 (Luxembourg Francs). If the annual turnover does not exceed Lfrs 1,000,000, certain deductions are allowed.

In broad terms, 'business' means any activity, including any trade, profession or vocation, carried on with a reasonable degree of continuity and organisation, whether profit-making or not.

RATES OF TAX

The current standard rate of VAT is 12%.

Principal supplies	*Rate*
Special reduced rate	3%
Agriculture and forestry; basic food and medicine.	
Reduced rate	6%
Food; books, magazines and printed matter; fuel and power; medical supplies and medicine; tobacco; original paintings, engravings, sculptures; transport of persons; cultural and social services; refrigeration, heat and steam.	
Standard rate	12%
All other taxable supplies.	

Certain supplies of goods are taxable but carry a zero rate; others are exempt from VAT altogether.

The main types of zero-rated supplies are as follows:

- exports;
- transborder transport;
- processing of export supplies; and
- certain financial transactions and insurance.

The following are the main types of exempt supplies:

- certain land transactions;

- insurance;
- financial transactions;
- education;
- health;
- imports of airplanes and ships;
- importation of IOU notes, bonds, shares, banknotes excluding collector's items; and
- imports of gold bars and gold coins being legal tender and excluding collector's items.

TAX INVOICES

When a registered person supplies goods or services to another he must issue a tax invoice. The recipient must retain this in order to claim input tax. Tax invoices must show amongst other things:

- tax point;
- supplier's name and address;
- customer's name and address;
- type of supply;
- rate of tax; and
- total tax chargeable.

If the customer agrees, a less detailed invoice for supplies not exceeding Lfr 2,000 in value may be issued.

PLACE OF SUPPLY

The distinction between whether a supply is one of goods or one of services is important because the rules governing the time and place of supply are different and, on occasions, may decide whether the supply is taxable or not, or taxed at a zero or positive rate.

Supply of goods

The principle is that goods are supplied wherever they are located when the power of disposal is transferred.

Supply of services

The principle is that services are supplied at the entrepreneur's place of business but there are exceptions.

For transportation services the place of supply is every place along the route taken during transport. Where a transport service is rendered proportionate between points inside and outside Luxembourg, a part of the service is treated as being supplied in Luxembourg, and the remainder being supplied outside Luxembourg. Auxiliary services in connection with transport are deemed to be supplied at the place where they are physically carried out.

REGISTRATION

Any person (entrepreneur) who engages in economic activities in an independent and regular way with the intention of producing income (not necessarily profit) must register for VAT from the start of his activities regardless of the scope of the results or the place of the activities. The only exceptions are as follows:

- agricultural and forestry entrepreneurs who are taxed under a special regime; and
- entrepreneurs supplying only certain exempt goods and services which do not give rise to any deduction of VAT.

Small entrepreneurs who are exempt from VAT must still register, and so must non-resident entrepreneurs who do not have a permanent establishment in Luxembourg but who perform taxable transactions there, that is if they supply or are deemed to supply goods or services in Luxembourg (see above).

In addition, non-resident entrepreneurs may be required to appoint a representative in Luxembourg and/or make a security deposit. Such a representative will be held jointly and severally liable with his principal for the fulfilment of all VAT obligations, including the payment of VAT and penalties. Such a representative must be a resident of Luxembourg.

There is no facility to register companies as a group in Luxembourg.

IMPORTATION PROCEDURES

The importation of goods is subject to VAT but importations of services are not taxable. Where the VAT on import becomes payable by a registered taxpayer, the actual collection of VAT due is postponed and VAT due at importation can be included on the normal VAT return. However, where the VAT is due from a non-resident entrepreneur without a permanent establishment in Luxembourg he may be required to appoint a representative. The representative can be held liable to pay any VAT fines due from the non-resident entrepreneur and takes his place in all matters connected with VAT law. A security deposit or bank guarantee may also be required.

INPUT TAX DEDUCTION

The normal rule is that possession of a tax invoice is essential to substantiate a claim to deduct input tax, that is VAT incurred on business expenditure. Only the person to whom the supply is made is entitled to claim input tax deduction; this may not necessarily be the person who pays for the supply. If goods are used only partly for business purposes, only VAT on the proportion attributable to business use may be claimed. VAT incurred on certain goods and services is non-deductible.

A person who makes only exempt supplies, however, is not entitled to register at all and therefore cannot claim any VAT as input tax. A registered person who makes both taxable and exempt supplies may be entitled to only a pro rata recovery of his input tax depending on the application of certain complex rules regarding partial exemption.

Services into countries outside the EC such as those of a bank granting loans to customers in non-EC countries are deemed to be exports which give a proportional claim for tax deduction.

ADMINISTRATION

VAT is administered by the Administration de l'Enregistrement des Domaines. In order to enforce the collection of VAT and to increase the accuracy of VAT return details the tax authorities are entitled to impose fines up to Lfrs 50,000. Serious fiscal offences might even be punished with imprisonment.

APPEALS

The taxable person may appeal against a decision of the tax authority which completely or partly dismisses the claim within three months of the decision being made. Appeals are heard by the Luxembourg Civil Court.

VAT AND OTHER TAXES

A person who cannot recover input tax, for example because he makes only exempt supplies, can treat the irrecoverable VAT element as part of the cost for other tax purposes. This applies also to those registered persons who may only be entitled to partial VAT recovery due to partial exemption.

VAT REFUND PROCEDURES

Entrepreneurs resident in the European Community

1 Can a claim for a refund be made by the entrepreneur direct to the Luxembourg tax authorities?
Yes. The claim may be made direct by the non-resident person or by his appointed agent.

2 To what address should the claim be made?
L'Administration de l'Enregistrement et des Domaines
Service de Remboursement TVA
1–3 av Guillaume
BP 1004
1010 Luxembourg.

3 Which form should be submitted and in which language should it be completed?
The claimant may use the Luxembourg form TVA 26–3 86–4M–73338 obtainable from the address above or any of the standard forms used throughout the EC. Whichever version of the form is used it must be completed in either French or German.

4 What are the minimum amounts that may be reclaimed and how frequently can such claims be submitted?
The general rules relating to time and cash limits are set out in the introduction. The minimum amounts, which may be claimed from the Luxembourg authorities are as follows:

	Minimum claim
	Lfrs
Calendar year claim	1,100
Intermediate claim	9,000
Claim for remainder of calendar year	1,100

5 What is the time limit for submitting a claim?
The claim must be made within six months of the end of the calendar year.

6 Is any Luxembourg VAT not reclaimable?
VAT cannot, in general, be reclaimed in respect of expenses incurred by an entrepreneur where his business would by its

nature be treated as exempt if he was carrying it on in the country of the claim. An example of this is VAT on expenses incurred by an insurance company representative.

7 Which documents must be submitted with the repayment claim form?

The official claim form must be accompanied by a certificate of status, obtainable from the claimant's own tax authorities, proving that the claimant is registered for VAT in a member state, and the original invoices. The invoices will be stamped and returned, normally within three months.

8 How long, on average, will the authorities take to repay the amount claimed?

The authorities must make a refund within six months of receiving a satisfactory claim. In practice, claims are repaid within three or four months. If a claim is not satisfactory, delays will occur while enquiries are made of the claimant.

9 Is it necessary to appoint a fiscal representative in Luxembourg and, if not, is it advisable to do so?

Claims may be made direct to the Luxembourg tax authorities at the address above by the non-resident claimant or his non-resident appointed agent. Although there may be no requirement to appoint a Luxembourg agent to submit claims, an agent may well be able to assist in preparing proper claims and obtaining refunds as quickly as possible.

Entrepreneurs not resident in the European Community

10 Does the ability to make a claim also apply to non-EC entrepreneurs?

Repayments of Luxembourg VAT will be made to non-EC entrepreneurs if there is a mutual agreement in existence between the non-EC state and Luxembourg.

11 Is the procedure the same as for entrepreneurs resident in the EC?

In general, the procedure is the same as for entrepreneurs resident in the EC. However, the claim can be made only once a year and the minimum amount that may be reclaimed is Lfrs 4,500 a year.

11 The Netherlands

SCOPE OF THE TAX

Value Added Tax (VAT) was introduced on 1 January 1969 to replace purchase tax. The legislation was substantially amended with effect from 1 January 1979 in accordance with the EC Sixth VAT Directive.

The VAT code applies throughout Dutch territory in Europe.

VAT is charged on:

- the supply of goods or services made in the Netherlands which is a taxable supply, made by an entrepreneur, in the course or furtherance of a business;
- the importation of goods into the Netherlands by any person (not only an entrepreneur).

The term 'services' includes all activities which do not qualify as supplies of goods.

An entrepreneur is any person (individual, partnership, company, association, etc) who carries out a business, trade or profession, to fulfil economic needs in society, with a reasonable degree of continuity and organisation, whether profitable or profit-making or not.

The exploitation of goods (the leasing of immovable property for example) is also deemed to be a business activity.

Most business transactions in the Netherlands are therefore liable to VAT and are called 'taxable supplies'. Only small entrepreneurs, that is those whose annual VAT payable after input tax deduction is less than Dfl 2,174 (excluding corporate bodies) can stay outside the scope of the tax. Special arrangements have been made for farmers. VAT is also chargeable on goods taken by the entrepreneur for personal use. VAT is not charged on 'self supplies' in general, but if goods are produced for internal purposes in respect of exempt or partly-exempt businesses, VAT must be accounted for on the open markct value or production cosl of such supplies.

VAT is levied on each individual import whether made by entrepreneurs or non-entrepreneurs. The VAT is calculated on the Customs value of the imported goods.

RATES OF TAX

The current standard rate of VAT is 18.5%. Certain supplies of goods and services are taxable, but carry a lower rate of 6%, others are exempt from VAT altogether.

The main types of reduced rate supplies are as follows, although it should be noted that there are numerous exceptions to the broad headings:

- agricultural products;
- food;
- books and magazines;
- medicine;
- passenger transport; and
- hotel accommodation.

The zero-rate applies in general to supplies of goods from outside the Netherlands which are not yet imported for customs purposes and to goods exported by an entrepreneur.

Exemptions

The main types of exempt supplies are as follows, but there are numerous exceptions to the broad headings:

- certain land and property transactions (with option facilities);
- health;
- education;
- insurance;
- financial transactions;
- radio and television;

- post, telegraph and telephone; and
- certain designated social and cultural services.

An exemption from VAT on the output means that input VAT is also non-deductible.

TAX INVOICES

When an entrepreneur supplies goods or services to another, he must issue a tax invoice. The recipient must retain this in order to reclaim input tax. Tax invoices must show, inter alia:

- the date of supply;
- a date and serial number;
- supplier's name and address;
- customer's name and address;
- an explicit description of the goods and services supplied;
- rate of tax; and
- total amount of tax chargeable.

If an entrepreneur delivers goods or renders services to non-entrepreneurs there is no obligation to issue invoices.

PLACE OF SUPPLY

The distinction between whether a supply is one of goods or one of services is important because the rules governing the time and place of supply are different and, on occasions, it may decide whether the supply is taxable or not, or taxed at a zero or positive rate.

Supplies of goods

The place of supply of goods depends on where the goods are when they are allocated or designated to a specific order from a customer. A supply takes place in the Netherlands if the specific goods to be supplied are located in the Netherlands. This applies even if the supplier has no place of business in the Netherlands or intends to export the goods to somewhere outside the Netherlands. For example, a US company may purchase goods located in the Netherlands for sale to another Dutch person or for export.

Alternatively, if the goods are outside the Netherlands at the time that they are allocated to a specific order, the supply takes place outside the Netherlands even if the supplier has a place of business within the Netherlands.

However, if the contract requires the supplier to process the goods in the Netherlands before the buyer takes property in the goods, the supply is made in the Netherlands. This is because a supply of processed goods is being made. The importation of the goods is a necessary preliminary step before the supply is made. Similarly, if a supplier installs or assembles goods in the Netherlands (eg machinery) the supply is made in the Netherlands.

Supplies of services

A supply of services is treated as taking place in the Netherlands if the supplier 'belongs' in the Netherlands. An entrepreneur is treated as belonging in the Netherlands if he has a business or some other fixed establishment in the Netherlands, such as an office, showroom, factory or warehouse.

If a business is carried out in the Netherlands through a branch or agency, the entrepreneur will be regarded as having a business establishment in the Netherlands. For example, an overseas architect who comes to the Netherlands and conducts his business from an office in Amsterdam would be regarded as belonging in the Netherlands in respect of those services.

The place where supplies of services are taxable is in general the place where the supplier belongs. There are, however, many types of services which are taxable at the place of taxability, ie the place where the recipient of the services resides. If the recipient is an entrepreneur this is the case amongst others with:

- supply of staff;
- financial services;
- advertising services;
- services of advisers (lawyers, chartered accountants, etc);
- leasing of tangible goods (except motorcars);
- licences and other rights.

This means, for example, that a lawyer in the US advising a Dutch company is rendering services which are taxable for VAT in the Netherlands.

Shifting of liability

To avoid the registration for VAT of foreign entrepreneurs who have no business, fixed establishment or branch in the Netherlands, the VAT liability is shifted to the recipient of the goods or services. So if for example a US lease-firm is hiring out computers to a Dutch company (a taxable service in the Netherlands), the US company does not have to register for VAT nor need it invoice VAT to the Dutch customer. The Dutch company has to file the VAT on its VAT return and can deduct that same amount of VAT as input tax, if it is entitled to reclaim VAT. If the Dutch customer in this case is a private hospital, the hospital has to charge the VAT on the lease terms itself and has to pay the tax because health organisations cannot deduct input tax (exempt output).

Note: This shifting of tax liability to the recipient does not apply in the case where the customer of the foreign supplier is a Dutch private person or a government body. In that case, the foreign entrepreneur has to register for VAT in the Netherlands if he carries out taxable supplies in the Netherlands.

REGISTRATION

All entrepreneurs, including permanent establishments of non-Dutch companies carrying on business in the Netherlands are required to register for VAT with the local VAT inspector.

Group treatment

Two or more Dutch resident companies or permanent establishments which are financially, structurally and economically connected in such a way that in practice they form a single economic unit, will be treated as a group for VAT purposes. Transactions between the members of the group are ignored and a single VAT return is filed by the representative member of the group on behalf of them all.

The criteria for a group registration are:

- *financial connection:* more than 50% of the working capital is in the hands of one person or company;
- *structural connection:* there is a clear leadership by a person or company over the group; and
- *economic connection:* the group members operate in the same market or the efforts of all members of the group are aimed at the same market.

Individual companies may, however, request treatment as independent companies on grounds of administrative convenience. Groups for VAT and corporation tax purposes do not have to contain the same members.

This can be used to produce tax advantages. For example, separate VAT groups for leasing and property companies can be set up inside a corporation tax group.

If there is a Dutch place of business

The registration will be made at the principal Dutch place of business and this address is to be entered on the VAT registration form. The VAT records and accounts should be kept and produced for inspection at that address. Someone at that address must be responsible for all VAT matters. If that person is an employee, he should normally be given written authority to act in this way.

If there is no Dutch place of business

The entrepreneur does not have to register for VAT if VAT liability for all supplies in the Netherlands is shifted to the receiving Dutch companies. If this is not the case the foreign entrepreneur has to register with Customs and Excise in Rijswijk (foreign entrepreneurs department). It is not necessary to appoint an agent but in practice it may help to simplify matters.

Foreign entrepreneurs who are not registered for VAT in the Netherlands can reclaim Dutch VAT on costs and expenses under the EC Eighth VAT Directive.

IMPORTATION PROCEDURES

Misunderstanding of the Dutch VAT importation procedures is a common source of errors and the following guidelines provide a brief, but not exhaustive, outline of the main principles:

If the place of supply is in the Netherlands

If the entrepreneur is registered for VAT in the Netherlands, he should be shown as the importer on the Customs entry.

He will be allowed to reclaim the VAT paid or deferred on importation of the goods as input tax subject to the normal rules. Any services supplied to the entrepreneur by an agent in arranging the supply can be zero-rated or standard-rated in which case the VAT may be reclaimed subject to the normal rules.

If the entrepreneur is not registered and does not supply any other goods or services within the Netherlands he can reclaim the VAT on importation under the EC Eighth Directive. In practice, it can be better to appoint a Dutch agent or have a branch in the Netherlands. The agent or branch will make the Custom's entry as the importer, pay or defer the VAT and take delivery of the goods. The agent or branch can reclaim this VAT as input tax, subject to the normal rules. When the agent passes on the goods in the Netherlands, he must treat the transaction as a supply by him and charge and account for VAT in the normal way.

If the place of supply is outside the Netherlands

Normally, the customer will import the goods and pay or defer the VAT on importation. Alternatively, if the entrepreneur has already sold goods to the Dutch customer on terms which require him or his Dutch agent to enter the goods and pay the VAT, only the customer can treat the VAT paid at importation as input tax.

The customer should be shown as consignee for VAT purposes on the Customs entry. The customer will then be issued with official evidence for input tax deduction.

Special arrangements

Dutch entrepreneurs who regularly import goods can ask their inspector for a licence to shift the liability to pay the VAT at the time and place of importation to the VAT return.

The entrepreneur is given an article 23 code number which can be used on Customs documents. This avoids the necessity of paying VAT at the time of importation. The VAT on importation has to be filed on the VAT return when the same amount of VAT can generally be deducted as input tax at the same time.

The actual payment of VAT on importation can also be suspended if goods are stored in Customs (bonded) warehouses. Exemptions can also apply for active processing, temporary importation and many other advantageous rules with regard to Customs duties, Excises and VAT.

There are special rules for goods from other Benelux countries. There is no need to have a licence in order to use the special arrangements.

INPUT TAX DEDUCTION

The normal rule is that possession of a tax invoice is essential to substantiate a claim to deduct input tax such as VAT incurred on business expenditure. Only the person to whom the supply is made is entitled to claim input tax deductions; this may not necessarily be the person who pays for the supply. If goods are used only partly for business purposes, only VAT on the proportion attributable to business use may be claimed. VAT incurred on certain goods and services is non-deductible, notably certain business entertainment expenses.

The input tax can also be disallowed under certain conditions for business or other gifts, supply to the entrepreneur's staff of housing, transportation, catering facilities and so on. VAT is fully deductible on expenses for hotel accommodation, car rental, petrol and the purchase of motor cars.

Subject to the non-deductible items mentioned above, a registered person who makes only taxable supplies is not restricted as to the amount of deductible input tax he may claim. A person who makes only exempt supplies, however, is not entitled to claim any VAT as input tax.

A registered person who makes both taxable and exempt supplies may be entitled only to a proportion of his input tax depending on the application of certain complex rules regarding partial exemption.

ADMINISTRATION

In the Netherlands VAT is administered by Customs and Excise and some specialised VAT offices. Automatic, and in some cases severe, financial penalties have been introduced into the system.

APPEALS

A taxpayer may appeal against a decision of the tax administration within two months after receipt of the notice. Appeals are dealt with by the local tax offices in the first instance. A second authority is the Court of Appeal (Tax Court) and, finally, cases can be heard in the Supreme (Tax) Court.

VAT AND OTHER TAXES

An entrepreneur who cannot recover input tax, for example because he only makes exempt supplies, can treat the irrecoverable VAT element as part of the cost for other tax purposes.

In the Netherlands a transfer tax is also levied on immovable property. Under certain conditions relief for this tax may apply if VAT is also levied on the same transfer.

VAT REFUND PROCEDURES

Entrepreneurs resident in the European Community

1 **Can a claim for a refund be made by the entrepreneur direct to the Dutch tax authorities?**
Yes. The claim may be made direct by the non-resident person or his appointed agent.

2 **To what address should the claim be made?**
The Inspecteur der Invoerrechten en Accijnzen
Postbus 5408
2280 HK Rijswijk.

3 **Which form should be submitted and in which language should it be completed?**
The claimant may use the Dutch form OB 97 obtainable from the address above or any of the standard forms used throughout the EC. Whichever version of the form is used it should be completed in Dutch, but in practice English or German versions are also accepted.

4 **What are the minimum amounts that may be reclaimed and how frequently can such claims be submitted?**
The general rules relating to time and cash limits are set out in the introduction. The minimum amounts which may be claimed from the Dutch authorities are as follows:

	Minimum claim
	1989
	Dfl
Calendar year claim	60
Intermediate claim	470
Claim for remainder of calendar year	60

5 **What is the time limit for submitting a claim?**
The claim must be made before the expiry of the six months following the end of the relevant calendar year. In practice, the Dutch authorities can accept a claim which is received after the six month limit. The refund is then made by discretion and no appeals can be made.

6 Is any Dutch VAT not reclaimable?
As explained above, VAT cannot, in general, be reclaimed in respect of expenses incurred by an entrepreneur where his business would by its nature be treated as exempt if he was carrying it on in the country of the claim. VAT is also non-deductible on expenses for food and beverages in restaurants, hotels and bars.

7 Which documents must be submitted with the repayment claim form?
The original invoices and a certificate of status, obtainable from his own tax authorities, proving that the claimant is registered for VAT in a member state, must accompany the official claim form.

8 How long, on average, will the authorities take to repay the amount claimed?
The authorities must make a refund within six months of receiving a satisfactory claim. In practice, claims are repaid well within this limit. If a claim is not satisfactory, delays will occur whilst enquiries are made of the claimant.

9 Is it necessary to appoint a fiscal representative in the Netherlands and, if not, is it advisable to do so?
Claims may be made direct to the Dutch tax authorities at the address above by the non-resident claimant or by his appointed agent. Although there is no requirement to appoint a Dutch agent to submit claims, an agent may well be able to assist in preparing proper claims and obtaining refunds as quickly as possible.

Entrepreneurs not resident in the European Community

10 Does the ability to make a claim also apply to non-EC entrepreneurs?
Yes. It is possible for non-EC entrepreneurs to make a claim.

11 Is the procedure the same as for entrepreneurs resident in the EC?
The procedure is largely the same; the same forms can be used, and it is also advisable to send a certificate to prove the status of

the entrepreneur from the claimant's own tax authorities. If the claimant has no VAT registration number in the country concerned a footnote must be made to explain the absence of this number (this will normally be because there is no VAT legislation in the country).

12 Portugal

SCOPE OF THE TAX

Value Added Tax was introduced in Portugal on 1 January 1986 to replace sales transactions tax. With the introduction of VAT, sales transactions tax, tourism tax, stamp tax (on certain transactions) and railroad tax were abolished.

For VAT purposes the Portuguese territory comprises continental Portugal and the islands of the Azores and Madeira.

Taxation is centrally administered by the 'Direccao-Geral das Contribuicoes e Impostos' (DGCI), an autonomous department of the Ministry of Finance.

The 'Servico de Administracao do IVA' (SIVA) is the section inside the DGCI which has overall charge of the imposition, regulation and collection of VAT in Portugal.

VAT is charged on:

- the supply of goods or services in Portugal which is a taxable supply made by a taxable person in the course or furtherance of a business;
- the importation of goods into Portugal by any person (not only a taxable person); and
- the importation of certain types of services into Portugal by a taxable person.

Most business transactions in Portugal are therefore liable to VAT and are called 'taxable supplies'. A person who makes taxable supplies above a certain value (Esc 500,000 if he exercises a recognised liberal profession defined in an appendix to the Professional Tax Code or Esc 800,000 if he is subject to industrial tax) is called a 'taxable person' and must be registered for VAT.

RATES OF TAX

VAT is applied at three different rates. The current standard rate is
17%.

Principal supplies	*Rate*
Reduced rate	8%

Reduced rate
Some food, wine, beer, education and educational
materials, energy, raw materials for textile industry,
supplies of services.

Normal rate	17%
Increased rate	30%

Increased rate
Luxury items including furs, spirits, firearms and
aircraft.

The rates applied to goods sold and services rendered in the
Azores and Madeira and to imports cleared through Customs in
those locations have been fixed at 6%, 12% and 21% respectively.
Certain supplies of goods and services are taxable but carry a
zero-rate; others are exempt from VAT altogether.

The main types of zero-rated supplies are as follows, although it
should be noted that there are numerous exceptions:

- food;
- books, magazines and printed matter;
- water;
- agricultural tools;
- cinema tickets; and
- pharmaceutical products.

The following are the main types of exempt supply, although again
it should be noted that there are numerous exceptions:

- services rendered by lawyers, medical doctors, interpreters,
  and so on;
- insurance;
- banking and financial transactions;
- education;
- health; and
- real estate transfers.

TAX INVOICES

When a registered person supplies goods or services to another, he must issue a tax invoice. The recipient must retain this in order to reclaim input tax. Tax invoices must show:

- serial number;
- tax point;
- supplier's name, address and fiscal number;
- customer's name, address and fiscal number;
- type of supply;
- rate of tax; and
- total tax chargeable.

PLACE OF SUPPLY

The distinction between whether a supply is one of goods or one of services is important because the rules governing the time and place of supply are different and, on occasions, it may decide whether the supply is taxable or not, or taxed at a zero or positive rate.

Supplies of goods

The place of supply of goods depends on where the goods are when they are allocated or designated to a specific order from a customer. A supply takes place in Portugal if the specific goods to be supplied are located in Portugal. This applies even if the supplier has no place of business in Portugal or intends to export the goods to somewhere outside Portugal. For example, a US company may purchase goods located in Portugal for sale to another Portuguese person or for export.

Alternatively, if the goods are outside Portugal at the time that they are allocated to a specific order, the supply takes place outside Portugal even if the supplier has a place of business within Portugal.

However, if the contract requires the supplier to process the goods in Portugal before the buyer takes property in the goods, the supply is made in Portugal. This is because a supply of processed goods is being made. The importation of the goods is a necessary preliminary step before the supply is made. Similarly, if a supplier installs or assembles goods in Portugal the supply is made in Portugal.

Supplies of services

A supply of services is treated as taking place in Portugal if the supplier 'belongs' in Portugal. An entrepreneur is treated as belonging in Portugal if he has a business or some other fixed establishment in Portugal, such as an office, showroom, factory or mobile workshop. If a business is carried out in Portugal through a branch or agency, the entrepreneur will be regarded as having a business establishment in Portugal. If the entrepreneur has business establishments in more than one country and supplies services, each supply made will be looked at separately and the entrepreneur will be regarded as belonging in the country where the establishment most closely concerned with the particular supply is located. For example, if the Portuguese branch of an overseas company is more directly concerned with a particular supply of services than the head office overseas, the place of supply is Portugal and, if applicable, the supply is subject to Portuguese VAT.

Overseas residents who supply services, but have no business or other establishment in any country, belong in the country where they have their usual place of residence and the supplies of services will be outside the scope of Portuguese VAT. The usual place of residence of a company is the place where it is legally constituted.

Goods or services transferred between different parts of a single company are normally disregarded for the purposes of Portuguese VAT. However, if in the course of carrying on a business in Portugal, goods are transferred or services are provided from Portugal to an entrepreneur's place of business outside Portugal, the transfers to the overseas place of business will be treated as a zero-rated supply so long as no other taxable supplies are made in Portugal. The zero-rating provision applies whether the main place of business is inside or outside Portugal. It enables an entrepreneur, who would not otherwise be a taxable person, to be registered in Portugal and claim repayment of input tax. This provision assists overseas traders who transfer stock from Portugal to their overseas place of business. It can also help an overseas trader who makes no other taxable supplies but maintains a representative office in Portugal which provides services to a head office or branch operating outside Portugal.

REGISTRATION

Persons who make or expect to make taxable supplies in Portugal, under the above rules, of more than Esc 125,000 if exercising a recognised liberal profession or Esc 200,000 if subject to industrial tax, in a calendar quarter or respectively Esc 500,000 or Esc 800,000 in a year are required to register for VAT with the Direccao-Geral das Contribuicoes e Impostos (SIVA).

Where two or more Portuguese resident companies are under common control they may elect to be registered as a single group for VAT purposes so that transactions between members of the VAT group are ignored and only one VAT return is made by the group.

The following rules determine where an entrepreneur will be registered for VAT.

If there is a Portuguese place of business

The registration will be made at the principal Portuguese place of business and this address is to be entered on the VAT registration form. The VAT records and accounts should be kept and produced for inspection at that address. Someone at that address must be responsible for all VAT matters.

If there is no Portuguese place of business

The entrepreneur may appoint an agent to act for him in VAT matters by letter of authority. Registration will then be made at the agent's address. The agent may be a company, a firm or an individual resident in Portugal. Sufficient information must be given to the agent to enable him to keep VAT accounts, make returns and pay tax on the entrepreneur's behalf on a continuing basis. An agent appointed in this way must keep separate VAT accounts and make separate VAT returns for his principal, in addition to those in respect of any VAT registration of his own.

If the entrepreneur has an employee who operates from a private address in Portugal, authority to deal with VAT matters may be given to that person.

If a VAT agent or a Portuguese based employee cannot be

appointed, the Portuguese customer must be responsible for all VAT matters.

IMPORTATION PROCEDURES

Misunderstanding of the Portuguese VAT importation procedures is a common source of error and the following guidelines provide a brief, but not exhaustive, outline of the main principles:

If the place of supply is in Portugal

If the entrepreneur is registered for VAT in Portugal, he should be shown as the importer on the Customs entry. He will be allowed to reclaim the VAT paid or deferred on importation of the goods as input tax subject to the normal rules. Any services supplied to the entrepreneur by an agent in arranging the supply will be standard-rated but this VAT may be reclaimed subject to the normal rules.

If the entrepreneur is not registered and does not supply any other goods or services within Portugal of a value exceeding the current registration limits, he can arrange for an agent who is resident in Portugal and who is registered for VAT purposes to import the goods on his behalf. Under this arrangement, the entrepreneur can avoid the need to be registered for Portuguese VAT solely in respect of supplies of imported goods.

The agent will make the Custom's entry as the importer, pay or defer the VAT and take delivery of the goods. The agent can reclaim this VAT as input tax, subject to the normal rules. When the agent passes on the goods in Portugal, he must treat the transaction as a supply by him and charge and account for VAT in the normal way. For this procedure to be operated, the entrepreneur must agree with the agent that he will issue a proper tax invoice for the supply. In these circumstances, the agent's supply of services to the entrepreneur arranging the supply of goods will be standard-rated, but the entrepreneur will not be able to recover the VAT that is charged because he is not registered for VAT in Portugal.

The adoption for VAT purposes of this arrangement does not affect the legal relationship between agent and principal for other purposes.

If the place of supply is outside Portugal

Normally the customer will import the goods and pay or defer the VAT on importation. Alternatively, if the entrepreneur has already sold goods to a Portuguese customer on terms which require him or his Portuguese agent to enter the goods and pay the VAT, only his customer can treat the VAT paid at importation as input tax. The customer should be shown as consignee for VAT purposes on the Customs entry. The customer will then be issued with official evidence for input tax deduction.

When an entrepreneur or his agent makes entry and pays the import VAT, the entrepreneur must not issue a tax invoice for this VAT since he is not making a taxable supply of the goods in Portugal. Any invoice which is issued should be suitably endorsed to make it clear that it is not a tax invoice and cannot be used as evidence for input tax, but is for recovery of a disbursement only.

INPUT TAX DEDUCTION

The normal rule is that possession of a tax invoice is essential to substantiate a claim to deduct input tax such as VAT incurred on business expenditure. Only the person to whom the supply is made is entitled to claim input tax deductions; this may not necessarily be the person who pays for the supply. If goods are used only partly for business purposes, only VAT on the proportion attributable to business use may be claimed. VAT incurred on certain goods and services is non-deductible, notably the purchase of new cars and certain business entertainment expenses.

Subject to the non-deductible items mentioned above, a registered person who makes only taxable supplies (whether at the standard rate and/or zero rate) is not restricted as to the amount of deductible input tax he may claim. A person who makes only exempt supplies, however, is not entitled to register at all and cannot therefore claim any VAT as input tax. A registered person who makes both taxable and exempt supplies may be entitled to only a proportion of his input tax depending on the application of certain complex rules regarding partial exemption.

ADMINISTRATION

Taxation is centrally administered by the Direccao-Geral das Contribuicoes e Impostos (DGCI), an autonomous department of the Ministry of Finance. The Servico de Administracao do IVA (SIVA) is the section inside the DGCI which has overall charge of the imposition, regulation and collection of VAT in Portugal.

The VAT Code includes a special chapter concerning the financial penalties which may be imposed if taxable persons either do not pay the tax or give misleading details to SIVA.

APPEALS

A person may appeal against a decision by the tax authorities. Appeals are heard by the tax authorities' tribunals in the first and second instance, and then by the Supreme Court.

VAT AND OTHER TAXES

A person who cannot recover input tax, for example because he makes only exempt supplies, can treat the irrecoverable VAT element as part of the cost for other tax purposes. This applies also to those registered persons who may only be entitled to partial VAT recovery due to partial exemption.

VAT REFUND PROCEDURES

Entrepreneurs resident in the European Community

1   **Can a claim for a refund be made by the entrepreneur direct to the Portuguese VAT authorities?**
    Yes. The claim may be made direct by the non-resident person.

2   **To what address should the claim be made?**
    Servico de Administracao do IVA
    Apartada 8121
    1802 Lisboa Codex.

3   **Which form should be submitted and in which language should it be completed?**
    The claimant should use the Portuguese form obtainable from the address above. That form must be completed in Portuguese.

4   **What are the minimum amounts that may be reclaimed and how frequently can such claims be submitted?**
    The general rules relating to time and cash limits are set out in the introduction. The minimum amounts which may be claimed from the Portuguese authorities are as follows:

	Minimum claim
	Esc
Calendar year claim	4,000
Intermediate claim (3 months)	32,000
Claim for remainder of calendar year	4,000

5   **What is the time limit for submitting a claim?**
    The claim must be made before the expiry of the six months following the end of the relevant calendar year. In practice the Portuguese authorities will accept any claim which is received on or before the last day of the six month period.

6   **Is any Portuguese VAT not reclaimable?**
    VAT cannot be reclaimed in respect of expenses incurred by an entrepreneur where his business would by its nature be treated as exempt if he were carrying it on in the country of the claim. VAT is also non-deductible on the purchase of new cars, expenditure on transport, hotel accommodation and on certain business entertainment expenses.

7 Which documents must be submitted with the repayment claim form?
A certificate of status, obtainable from the tax authorities, proving that the claimant is registered for VAT in a member state, and the original invoices must accompany the official claim form. The invoices will be stamped and returned normally within one month.

8 How long, on average, will the authorities take to repay the amount claimed?
The authorities must make a refund within six months of receiving a satisfactory claim. In practice, claims are repaid well within this limit. If a claim is not satisfactory, delays will occur whilst enquiries are made of the claimant.

9 Is it necessary to appoint a fiscal representative in Portugal and, if not, is it advisable to do so?
Claims may be made direct to the Portuguese tax authorities at the address above by the non-resident claimant or his non-resident appointed agent. Although there is no requirement to appoint a Portuguese agent to submit claims an agent may well be able to assist in preparing proper claims and obtaining refunds as quickly as possible.

Entrepreneurs not resident in the European Community

10 Does the ability to make a claim also apply to non-EC entrepreneurs?
Yes. An entrepreneur registered for business purposes in a non-EC country can use the scheme to reclaim VAT paid in Portugal, provided that:

- he is not registered, liable or eligible to be registered for VAT in Portugal;
- he has no place of business or other residence in the Community;
- he is subject to a tax on the transaction in his country; and
- the non-EC country assures a similar treatment in relation to a Portuguese entrepreneur.

11   Is the procedure the same as for entrepreneurs resident in the EC?

In general, the procedure is similar. However, the Portuguese authorities require that the claim is submitted through a tax representative resident in Portugal appointed by letter of authority with necessary powers for the claim.

13 Spain

SCOPE OF THE TAX

The 'Impuesto sobra el Valor Anadido' (IVA) was introduced on 1 January 1986 on the entry of Spain into the European Community. The tax replaced a range of 24 other taxes or duties notably the 'Impuesto General sobre el Trafico de Empresas' (IGTE or sales tax) and the 'Impuesto sobre el Lujo' (Luxury Tax).

For the purposes of VAT, Spain comprises peninsular Spain and the Balearic Islands. The Canary Islands as well as the North Africa enclaves of Ceuta and Melilla are excluded from the territory of application of IVA.

VAT is charged on:

- the supply of goods or services made in Spain which is a taxable supply and made by a 'sujeto pasivo' or taxable person in the course or furtherance of a business;
- the importation of goods into Spain by any person regardless of whether it is in the course of a business.

The supply of goods and services taxable under VAT are those carried out by businesses or professionals in the course of their habitual or occasional activities.

The concept of supply of goods includes not only those operations which constitute an evident transfer of goods but also those of an analogous nature including transactions which are deemed to be self-supplies.

The concept of supply of services has a residual definition within the context of Spanish VAT; that is, it is intended to cover all transactions not previously dealt with under 'supply of goods' unless specifically defined as exempt.

Exemptions under VAT whether in the supply of goods or in the supply of services cover both internal and external operations with specific reference to the list of transactions contained in the Sixth EC Directive.

Imports are considered as taxable regardless of the legal personality of the importer (individuals, businessmen, professionals or companies). Imports are defined as the entry of goods into mainland Spain or the Balearic Islands regardless of their origin, thus treating imports from the Canaries and Ceuta and Melilla as imports for the purposes of VAT.

RATES OF TAX

The current standard rate of VAT is 12%, with a lower rate of 6% and an increased rate of 33%.

Principal supplies	*Rate*
Reduced rate Food for both animal and human consumption, books, newspapers and magazines, medical supplies and treatment, invalid vehicles, housing, education and educational material, and transport, hotels, camping and restaurants (except five star hotels and top category restaurants which are subject to standard rate), shows and the like, urban cleaning services, commercial fairs and exhibitions.	6%
Standard rate Applied to all transactions except those specifically treated as taxable under another rate or exempt.	12%
Higher rate Cars, pleasure boats, jewellery, precious stones and gold and silver objects, luxury clothing.	33%

Exemptions
The main exemptions are:

- social services such as medical assistance, education, sports facilities and the postal service;
- cultural activities; and
- insurance and financial transactions.

TAX INVOICES

When a 'sujeto pasivo' makes a taxable supply of goods or services to another, the taxable person must issue an invoice which meets the formal requirements established for the tax. The recipient must retain the invoice in order to reclaim the IVA charged thereon. The minimum information that must be shown on a tax invoice is as follows:

- invoice and serial number;
- supplier's name, address and tax number;
- customer's name, address and tax number (or personal identity number in the case of an individual);
- the nature of the transaction;
- the rate of tax;
- amount of tax charged; and
- the place and date of issue.

When a customer cannot reclaim the tax and the total amount of the invoice does not exceed Ptas 10,000 then it is not necessary to identify the name and address of the customer.

PLACE OF SUPPLY

There are different rules governing the place of supply of goods and the place of supply of services and these may determine whether the supply is taxable or not or the responsibility for paying over the tax.

Supplies of goods

In general, all non-exempt supplies of goods made within the Spanish territory will be subject to VAT, the warehouse or factory from which the goods leave being deemed the point of supply. The supply of property is considered to take place where the property is situated.

If the supply of goods requires installation or assembly then the place of destination of the goods will be considered to be the point of supply if the installation or assembly represents more than 15% of the total amount of the supply.

Supplies of services

The general rule concerning the supply of services is that they will be considered to be carried out where the supplier of the services has his business or permanent establishment in accordance with the OECD definition.

Special rules apply to the supply of certain types of services. In the case of property it is considered that any services directly related to property, such as those of an architect or management or negotiation services, are carried out in the place where the property is situated. Transport services are considered to be carried out in accordance with the part of the journey using Spanish territory or airspace or territorial waters. Cultural activities, hotel services and repair services are considered to be supplied where they are materially carried out.

Finally, the supply of certain types of services is considered to be carried out in the usual place of residence of the recipient of the services. This special rule applies in particular to industrial or intellectual property rights, publicity, engineering services, advisory services, supply of information, insurance and financial services and the rental of movable tangible assets.

REGISTRATION

All businesses, traders or professionals carrying out an activity which is subject to the tax in Spain are obliged to register for VAT purposes. This will apply to non-resident entrepreneurs with a permanent establishment in Spain but those without a permanent establishment are not treated as taxable persons for VAT purposes and do not have to register. However, an entrepreneur who is established in the Canaries, Ceuta, Melilla or another EC country must appoint a resident representative if he wishes to claim refunds of Spanish VAT.

Registered persons are obliged to maintain specific books of account to register invoices received, invoices issued and invoices relating to the acquisition of fixed assets.

There are exceptions in respect of the formal books of account in the case of certain special groups of traders such as farmers and small retailers.

Groups of companies must register separately if they are separate legal entities even if they are owned or controlled by one person but a multi-divisional organisation may register as one entrepreneur.

IMPORTATION PROCEDURES

All normal imports are subject to IVA, the taxable event being considered as 'the definitive or temporary entry of goods into the territory of application of the tax, whatever the finality of the importation or the nature of the importer'. It is normal for a Customs agent to arrange the importation and to pay the VAT due on the goods imported.

There are a number of exceptions which apply to the temporary importation of aircraft and boats etc involved in international transport. Other exceptions cover the importation of personal goods on change of residence and the importation of material for commercial inspection such as samples, catalogues and publicity articles.

In the case of temporary imports or imports made for the purposes of further processing prior to re-exportation then the tax may be suspended, usually with the provision of a bank guarantee.

INPUT TAX DEDUCTION

Input tax is deductible by registered persons provided certain conditions are met. Principally, it is necessary for the registered person to be in possession of the tax invoice or equivalent document and to have accounted for the same in the register of invoices received.

VAT incurred on certain items is non-deductible; in particular VAT may not be recovered on:

- the acquisition of cars;
- travel or hotel and entertaining expenses;
- acquisitions subject to the increased rate of tax.

Certain taxable persons may be partially or totally exempt for the purposes of VAT and this will affect their right to deduct the input tax. The general rule is that VAT may be deducted provided that the input tax is deductible and that it corresponds to tax on goods or services acquired for carrying out operations which are in turn subject to and not exempt from VAT as well as others which are related to exports.

Partially exempt persons may only deduct the tax that is incurred on the supply of goods or services when these are used to make taxable supplies of goods or services rendered. Where a taxable person is partially exempt he may opt for the application of a specific pro rata method in order to reclaim the percentage of input tax that corresponds to the acquisition of goods and services used in producing outputs subject to the tax. Subject to the approval of the tax authorities one may apply an alternative method known as the general pro rata for the purpose of determining the amount of input tax which is deductible.

Exporters whose annual export figures exceed Ptas 20,000,000 are entitled to receive their refunds at the end of each quarter.

ADMINISTRATION

The administration of VAT is the responsibility of the Ministerio de Economia y Hacienda.

APPEALS

Appeals against a decision by the tax authorities in respect of VAT may be made in the first instance through the administrative route. If this level of appeal fails then an appeal may be taken to a 'Tribunal Economico Administrativo', a court connected with the Ministry of Economy and Finance. The ultimate recourse in the appeal process follows a procedure known as 'contencioso-administrativo' through the courts of justice.

VAT AND OTHER TAXES

A taxable person who is unable to use the VAT incurred on purchases of goods and services, either because the transaction is specifically treated as one which does not give the right to recover the tax or because the taxable person makes only exempt or partially exempt supplies, may treat the non-recovered tax as part of the cost for the purposes of other taxes such as corporate tax or income tax.

VAT REFUND PROCEDURES

Entrepreneurs resident in the European Community

1 Can a claim for a refund be made by the entrepreneur direct to the Spanish tax authorities?
Yes. The claim may be made directly by the non-resident person.

2 To what address should the claim be made?
Delgacion de Hacienda Especial de Madrid
Seccion de Regimenes Especiales
Calle Guzman el Bueno 139, Planta 2
28071 Madrid.

3 Which form should be submitted and in which language should it be completed?
The claimant may use the form Mod 361 or any of the standard forms throughout the EC. There is also a form 351 for the use of claimants resident in the Canary Islands and the Spanish enclaves of Ceuta and Melilla in North Africa for whom a similar scheme is in operation. Whichever version of the forms is used it must be completed in Spanish.

4 What are the minimum amounts that may be reclaimed and how frequently can such claims be submitted?
The general rules relating to time and cash limits are set out in the introduction. The minimum amounts which may be claimed from the Spanish tax authorities are as follows:

	Minimum claim
	Ptas
Calendar year claim	3,000
Intermediate claim	25,000
Claim for remainder of calendar year	3,000

5 What is the time limit for submitting a claim?
The claim must be made before the expiry of the six months following the end of the relevant calendar year.

6 Is any Spanish VAT not reclaimable?
VAT may be reclaimed when the tax has been incurred on the acquisition or import of goods and services to be used exclusively in those transactions which give rise to the right to

refund. In the same way that the VAT law restricts the right of resident taxable persons to deduct input tax on the supply of certain goods and services, so these restrictions also apply to the claim procedure. The transactions for which VAT may not be reclaimed are as follows:

- the purchase of private motor vehicles and the related expenses incurred in respect of hire or maintenance and so on (except public or freight transport);
- travel expenses of the taxable person and his staff or third parties;
- hotel, restaurant and entertaining expenses;
- the purchase of luxury items taxed at the higher rate; and
- entertaining clients or the provision of gifts to clients.

7   Which documents must be submitted with the repayment claim form?
A certificate of status issued by the tax authorities in the claimant's own country proving that he is registered for VAT in that country and stating the VAT registration number if applicable, plus the original invoices and other relevant documents.

8   How long, on average, will the authorities take to repay the amount claimed?
The authorities must process the claim within the five months following the date of presentation and notify the claimant within 30 days of completing the processing.

9   Is it necessary to appoint a fiscal representative in Spain and, if not, is it advisable to do so?
No. It is not necessary for a claimant resident in the EC to appoint a fiscal representative who is resident in Spain.

Entrepreneurs not resident in the European Community

10   Does the ability to make a claim also apply to non-EC entrepreneurs?
Yes. An entrepreneur registered for business purposes in a non-EC country can use the scheme to reclaim VAT paid in Spain provided that reciprocal treatment exists for Spanish entrepreneurs or professionals in that country.

11 Is the procedure the same as for entrepreneurs resident in the EC?

The claim procedure is identical to that which applies for entrepreneurs resident in the EC except that a fiscal representative resident in Spain must be appointed. The tax authorities may require that the representative establish a guarantee in respect of the VAT reclaimed.

14 United Kingdom

SCOPE OF THE TAX

Value Added Tax (VAT) was introduced on 1 April 1973 to replace purchase tax. The legislation was substantially amended with effect from 1 January 1978 in accordance with the EC Sixth VAT Directive and is now contained mainly in the Value Added Tax Act 1983 (as amended), subsequent Finance Acts and Statutory Instruments issued by the Treasury from time to time.

For VAT purposes the UK comprises England, Scotland, Northern Ireland and Wales, while the Isle of Man has its own VAT law which is merged with the UK law. The Channel Islands have no VAT and are outside the EC for VAT purposes.

VAT is charged on:

- the supply of goods or services made in the UK which is a taxable supply, made by a taxable person, in the course or furtherance of a business;
- the importation of goods into the UK by any person (not only a taxable person);
- the importation of certain types of services into the UK by a taxable person.

The word 'supply' is not defined but it encompasses all types of supply – sale, hire purchase, hire, gift, loan, exchange and so on. Certain transactions are deemed to be supplies, some even to be self-supplies; others are deemed not to be supplies.

A 'taxable' person is any person (individual, partnership, company, trustee, club, association, charity, etc) who is registered for VAT or is required to be registered.

In broad terms 'business' means any activity, including any trade, profession or vocation, carried on with a reasonable degree of continuity and organisation, whether profitable or not, excluding a hobby or the provision of services by an employee to his employer.

Most business transactions in the UK are therefore liable to VAT and are called 'taxable supplies'. A person who makes taxable supplies above a certain value (above £25,400 from 21 March 1990) is called a 'taxable person' and must be registered for VAT.

RATES OF TAX

The current standard rate of VAT is 15%. Certain supplies of goods and services are taxable, but carry a zero-rate, others are exempt from VAT altogether.

The main types of zero-rated supplies are as follows, although it should be noted that there are numerous exceptions to the broad headings:

- food;
- books, magazines and printed matter;
- fuel and power, ie gas, electricity, etc when supplied to final consumers after 30 June 1990 but not petrol, diesel and oil for road use;
- new domestic buildings;
- certain international services;
- transport (excluding taxis and hire cars); and
- children's clothing and footwear.

The following are the main types of exempt supply, although it should again be noted that there are numerous exceptions:

- certain land transactions;
- insurance;
- financial transactions;
- education;
- health; and
- sports competitions.

Since 1 August 1989 most exempt property transactions have had a right of option to add tax at the standard rate of 15%.

TAX INVOICES

When a registered person supplies goods or services to another, he must issue a tax invoice. The recipient must retain this in order to reclaim input tax. Tax invoices must show inter alia;

- VAT registration number of supplier;
- tax point;
- date of supply;
- supplier's name and address;
- customer's name and address;
- type of supply;
- rate of tax;
- total tax chargeable expressed in sterling; and
- serial number.

If the customer agrees, a less detailed invoice for supplies not exceeding £50 in value may be issued.

PLACE OF SUPPLY

The distinction between whether a supply is one of goods or one of services is important because the rules governing the time and place of supply are different and, on occasions, it may decide whether the supply is taxable or not, or taxed at a zero or positive rate.

Supplies of goods

The place of supply of goods depends on where the goods are when they are allocated or designated to a specific order from a customer. A supply takes place in the UK if the specific goods to be supplied are located in the UK. This applies even if the supplier has no place of business in the UK or intends to export the goods to somewhere outside the UK. For example, a US company may purchase goods located in the UK for sale to another UK person or for export.

Alternatively, if the goods are outside the UK at the time that they are allocated to a specific order, the supply takes place outside the UK even if the supplier has a place of business within the UK.

For example, a US company may purchase goods in the Channel Islands for sale to another person within the Channel Islands.

However, if the contract requires the supplier to process the goods in the UK before the buyer takes property in the goods, the supply is made in the UK. This is because a supply of processed goods is being made. The importation of the goods is a necessary preliminary step before the supply is made. Similarly, if a supplier installs or assembles goods such as machinery in the UK the supply is made in the UK. If the supplier is not registered for VAT in the UK, Customs and Excise may exceptionally allow the supply of assembled or installed goods to be treated as being made outside the UK provided all of the following conditions are met:

- only a one-off supply is being made and no further business is expected in the UK at the time;
- the charges for the goods include any costs of assembly or installation;
- the customer acts as the importer for VAT purposes; and
- the full value of the supply (including assembly) is shown on the Customs import entry.

Supply of services

A supply of services is treated as taking place in the UK if the supplier 'belongs' in the UK. An entrepreneur is treated as belonging in the UK if he has a business or some other fixed establishment in the UK, such as an office, showroom, factory or mobile workshop. If a business is carried out in the UK through a branch or agency, the entrepreneur will be regarded as having a business establishment in the UK. If the entrepreneur has business establishments in more than one country and supplies services, each supply made will be looked at separately and the entrepreneur will be regarded as belonging in the country where the establishment most closely concerned with the particular supply is located. For example, if the UK branch of an overseas company is more directly concerned with a particular supply of services than the head office overseas, the place of supply is the UK and, if applicable, the supply is subject to UK VAT. Thus, an overseas architect who comes to the UK and conducts his business from an office in London would be regarded as belonging in the UK in respect of those services. Similarly, an entertainer who hires a theatre in the UK in order to give a performance is treated as belonging in the UK in respect of that performance and his services are liable to UK VAT.

Overseas residents who supply services, but have no business or other establishment in any country, belong in the country where they have their usual place of residence and the supplies of services will be outside the scope of UK VAT. The usual place of residence of a company is the place where it is legally constituted.

Goods or services transferred between different parts of a single legal entity, eg between branches of a single company, are normally disregarded for the purposes of UK VAT. If the UK branch of an overseas company does not make taxable supplies in the UK, it may still be able to register for UK VAT and obtain credit for VAT incurred on UK expenditure, but this will depend on the nature of the supplies made by the company as a whole. For example, a UK branch or representative office of an overseas company will be able to register for VAT if the supplies made by the overseas company outside the UK would have been subject to VAT (rather than exempt) if such supplies had been made in the UK. However, if the company's supplies outside the UK would have been exempt if they had been made in the UK, the UK branch or representative office will be unable to register for UK VAT.

REGISTRATION

Persons who make or expect to make taxable supplies in the UK under the above rules of more than £25,400 in a year are required to register for VAT with Customs & Excise.

Where two or more UK resident companies are under common control they may elect to be registered as a single group for VAT purposes so that transactions between members of the VAT group are ignored and only one VAT return is rendered for the group. For the purposes of 'residence' UK Customs & Excise accept that an overseas company may be treated as UK resident for VAT purposes if at least one full-time working director is resident in the UK and regularly attends board meetings of the company. The use of VAT groups is a major area of planning within the UK VAT system and it is important not only to plan the correct structure and content of a

VAT group or groups, but also to consider the direct tax implications of proposed VAT structures.

The following rules determine the place at which an overseas entrepreneur will be registered for VAT:

If there is a UK place of business

The registration will be made at the principal UK place of business and this address must be entered on the VAT registration form. The VAT records and accounts should be kept and produced for inspection at that address. Someone at that address must be responsible for all VAT matters. If that person is an employee, he should normally be given written authority to act in this way.

If there is no UK place of business

The entrepreneur may appoint an agent to act for him in VAT matters by letter of authority. Registration will then be made at the agent's address. The agent may be a company, a firm or an individual resident in the UK. Sufficient information must be given to the agent to enable him to keep VAT accounts, make returns and pay tax on the entrepreneur's behalf on a continuing basis. An agent appointed in this way must keep separate VAT accounts and make separate VAT returns for his principal, in addition to those in respect of any VAT registration of his own.

If the entrepreneur has an employee who operates from a private address in the UK, authority to deal with VAT matters may be given to that person.

If a VAT agent or a UK based employee cannot be appointed, and registration is to be at the entrepreneur's overseas address, UK Customs & Excise will normally require security to be lodged with them to cover anticipated VAT liabilities before effecting a VAT registration.

IMPORTATION PROCEDURES

Misunderstanding of the UK VAT importation procedures is a common source of error and the following guidelines provide a brief, but not exhaustive, outline of the main principles:

If the place of supply is in the UK

If the entrepreneur is registered for VAT in the UK, he should be shown as the importer on the Customs entry. He will be allowed to reclaim the VAT paid or deferred on importation of the goods as input tax subject to the normal rules. Any services supplied to the entrepreneur by an agent in arranging the supply will be standard-rated but this VAT may be reclaimed subject to the normal rules.

If the entrepreneur is not registered and does not supply any other goods or services within the UK of a value exceeding the current registration limits he can arrange for an agent who is resident in the UK and who is registered for VAT purposes to import the goods on his behalf. Under this arrangement, the entrepreneur can avoid the need to be registered for UK VAT solely in respect of supplies of imported goods.

For this procedure to be operated, the agent will make the Custom's entry as the importer, pay or defer the VAT and take delivery of the goods. The agent can reclaim this VAT as input tax, subject to the normal rules. When the agent passes on the goods in the UK, he must treat the transaction as a supply by him and charge and account for VAT in the normal way. For this procedure to operate, the entrepreneur must agree with the agent that he, the agent, will issue a proper tax invoice for the supply. In these circumstances, the agent's supply of services to the entrepreneur in arranging the supply of goods will be standard-rated, but the entrepreneur will not be able to recover the VAT that is charged because he is not registered for VAT in the UK.

Adopting this arrangement for VAT purposes does not affect the legal relationship between agent and principal for other purposes.

If the place of supply is outside the UK

Normally, the customer will import the goods and pay or defer the VAT on importation. Alternatively, if the entrepreneur has already sold goods to a UK customer on terms which require him or his UK agent to enter the goods and pay the VAT, only his customer can treat the VAT paid at importation as input tax. The customer should be shown as consignee for VAT purposes on the Customs entry. The customer will then be issued with official evidence to substantiate his input tax deduction. A copy of the entry will be required with the following declaration in the supplementary information box: 'goods imported on behalf of . . . VAT registration number . . .'

When an entrepreneur or his agent enters goods into the UK and pays the import VAT, the entrepreneur must not issue a tax invoice for this VAT since he is not making a taxable supply of the goods in the UK. Any invoice which is issued should be suitably endorsed to make it clear that it is not a tax invoice and cannot be used as evidence for input tax, but is for recovery of a disbursement only.

Where the place of supply of the goods is outside the UK, an agent's supply of services to a person in arranging the supply of goods is zero-rated.

INPUT TAX DEDUCTION

The normal rule is that possession of a tax invoice is essential to substantiate a claim to deduct input tax such as VAT incurred on business expenditure. Only the person to whom the supply is made is entitled to claim input tax deductions; this may not necessarily be the person who pays for the supply. If goods are used only partly for business purposes, only VAT on the proportion attributable to business use may be claimed. VAT incurred on certain goods and services is non-deductible, notably the purchase of new cars and certain business entertainment expenses.

Subject to the non-deductible items mentioned above, a registered person who makes only taxable supplies (whether at the standard and/or zero-rate) is not restricted as to the amount of deductible input tax he may claim. A person who makes only exempt supplies, however, is not entitled to register at all and cannot therefore claim any VAT as input tax. A registered person who makes both taxable and exempt supplies may be entitled to claim only a proportion of his input tax depending on the application of certain complex rules regarding partial exemption.

ADMINISTRATION

The Treasury has overall charge of the imposition, regulation and collection of VAT in the UK. However, whereas direct taxes (for example corporation tax and income tax) are administered by the Inland Revenue, VAT is administered by the Customs and Excise – a body which has wide powers.

Failure to comply with the statutory requirements of VAT can result in the imposition of automatic financial penalties. Customs and Excise are empowered to impose penalties where an entrepreneur fails:

- to register for VAT at the correct time;
- either to send his VAT return or to pay the tax due thereon at the correct time; or
- to declare the correct amount of VAT due to be paid or repaid on his VAT return.

In addition to financial penalties, Customs and Excise will normally charge interest on any VAT that is not paid at the correct time. In most circumstances the penalty is applied automatically and Customs and Excise do not have any powers to reduce or mitigate it, regardless of whether the failure results from an innocent error or because the error arose from ignorance or misunderstanding of the law.

APPEALS

A person may appeal against a decision by Customs and Excise if it falls within certain defined categories. Appeals are heard by independent VAT Tribunals in the first instance but may then proceed, on a point of law only, to the High Court, Court of Appeal and House of Lords.

VAT AND OTHER TAXES

A person who cannot recover input tax, for example because he makes only exempt supplies, can treat the irrecoverable VAT element as part of the cost for other tax purposes. This applies also to those registered persons who may only be entitled to partial VAT recovery due to partial exemption.

VAT REFUND PROCEDURES

Entrepreneurs resident in the European Community

1 **Can a claim for a refund be made by the entrepreneur direct to the UK VAT authorities?**
Yes. The claim may be made direct by the non-resident person or his appointed agent.

2 **To what address should the claim be made?**
H M Customs and Excise
VAT Control Division C (Branch 2)
St John's House
Merton Road
Bootle
Merseyside
L20 3NN.

3 **Which form should be submitted and in which language should it be completed?**
The claimant may use the UK form VAT 65 obtainable from the address above or any of the standard forms used throughout the EC. Whichever version of the form is used it must be completed in English.

4 **What are the minimum amounts that may be reclaimed and how frequently can such claims be submitted?**
The general rules relating to time and cash limits are set out in the introduction. The minimum amounts that may be claimed from the UK authorities are as follows:

	Minimum claim £
Calendar year claim	16
Intermediate claim	130
Claim for remainder of calendar year	16

5 **What is the time limit for submitting a claim?**
The claim must be made before the expiry of the six months following the end of the relevant calendar year. In practice, the UK authorities will accept a claim which is received after the six month limit provided the postmark indicates that the claim was sent within the six month period.

6   Is any UK VAT not reclaimable?

As explained in the introduction, VAT cannot, in general, be reclaimed in respect of expenses incurred by an entrepreneur where his business would by its nature be treated as exempt if he was carrying it on in the country of the claim. VAT is also non-deductible on the purchase of new cars and on certain business entertainment expenses.

7   Which documents must be submitted with the repayment claim form?

A certificate of status, obtainable from the tax authorities, proving that the claimant is registered for VAT in a member state, and the original invoices must accompany the official claim form. The invoices will be stamped and returned, normally within one month.

8   How long, on average, will the authorities take to repay the amount claimed?

The authorities must make a refund within six months of receiving a satisfactory claim. In practice, claims are repaid well within this limit. If a claim is not satisfactory, delays will occur whilst enquiries are made of the claimant.

9   Is it necessary to appoint a fiscal representative in the UK and, if not, is it advisable to do so?

Claims may be made direct to the UK tax authorities at the address above by the non-resident claimant or his non-resident appointed agent. Although there is no requirement to appoint a UK agent to submit claims, an agent may well be able to assist in preparing proper claims and obtaining refunds as quickly as possible.

Entrepreneurs not resident in the European Community

10   Does the ability to make a claim also apply to non-EC entrepreneurs?

Yes. An entrepreneur registered for business purposes in a non-EC country can use the scheme to reclaim VAT paid in the UK, provided that:

- he is not registered, liable or eligible to be registered for VAT in the UK;

- he has no place of business or other residence in the Community;
- no supplies are made in the UK other than transport services related to the international carriage of goods, or services where VAT is payable by the person in the UK to whom the supply is made.

It is a condition of the scheme that the entrepreneur's own country allows similar concessions to UK traders in respect of its own turnover taxes. However, a claim will only be refused on these grounds if that country has a scheme for refunding these taxes but refuses to allow UK traders to use it.

11 Is the procedure the same as for entrepreneurs resident in the EC?
In general the procedure is similar but the claim must be made no later than six months after the end of the 'prescribed year' in which the VAT was incurred. The prescribed year is the twelve months from 1 July to 30 June of the following calendar year, so you must make your claim no later than 31 December. Also, in certain circumstances, the UK authorities may require that a claim is submitted through a tax representative – an agent who is registered for VAT in the UK and established there.

Appendix 1

Specimen copy of a certificate of status and the standard refund claim form used in the UK

On the following pages we have included a specimen of the standard UK certificate of status and refund claim form. A certificate of status must be obtained from your own tax authorities to prove that you are registered for VAT in a member state of the EC other than the country from which you are claiming a refund.

A valid certificate of status must be submitted with the claim form or must already be held by the tax authorities in the member state from which you are claiming a refund.

As explained in the introductory section and in the country by country analysis a claim form, which is standard throughout the EC, printed in any official language of the EC may be used for making a refund claim, but whichever form is used it must be completed in the language of the country from which you are claiming.

Notes on completing the UK application form are included in Appendix 2.

The forms on the following pages are Crown Copyright and are reproduced by permission of the Controller of her Majesty's Stationery office.

Certificate of Status

HM Customs and Excise

CERTIFICATE OF STATUS OF
TAXABLE PERSON

The undersigned

....
(Name and address of competent authority)

certifies that

....
(Name of taxable person)

....

....
(Nature of activity)

....
(Address of the Establishment)

is a taxable person for the purposes of Value Added Tax, *his Registration
number being

Date ....

Office stamp

Signature.........................

....
(Name and grade)

*If the applicant does not have a Registration number, the competent authority
shall state the reason for this.

VAT 66   F 5037 (Nov. 1980)   S4995 (23983) Dd.8296368 50m 6/81 GWB.Ltd. Gp.870

UK claim form (page 1)

UK claim form (page 2)

Statement itemising VAT amounts relating to the period covered by this application

10

1) Each document submitted should be consecutively numbered starting with 1. The number should be inserted in the top right-hand corner of the face of the document. Enter details across the columns in respect of each invoice etc. submitted. If sufficient space is not available you must use a continuation sheet, headed with your tax registration number, endorsed Box 10 and attached firmly to the application form.

2) You are reminded that when tax is incurred by taxable persons who receive VAT group treatment, the group representative member must apply on behalf of all the members. As the supporting invoices produced will not necessarily be addressed to the representative member, the status certificate must also contain the names of those group members who incurred the tax.

Number	Nature of goods or services	Name, VAT Registration No. (if known) and address of supplier of goods or services	Date and number of invoice or import document	Amount of tax refund applied for	FOR OFFICIAL USE ONLY
				C/F	

CD 1223/1RW1(10.87)   Page 2.

UK claim form (page 3)

3)   Refunds of tax incurred may only be claimed subject to the rules of each state. Brief details of supplies in each member state on which tax
cannot be reclaimed are given in HM Customs and Excise Notice 723. Tax incurred on the following supplies will not be refunded by any member state:

(a)   supplies of goods which have been or are about to be exported; and

(b)   supplies to travel agents which are for the direct benefit of travellers. Under this scheme the term "travel agent "includes tour operators or
any person who purchases or re-supplies services to travellers.

Number	Nature of goods or services	Name, VAT Registration No. (if known) and address of supplier of goods or services	Date and number of invoice or import document	Amount of tax refund applied for	FOR OFFICIAL USE ONLY
			TOTAL B/F		
			Page 3.	TOTAL	

UK claim form (page 4)

Notes on Completion of the Application Form

A. General

The application must be made on the appropriate form, published in one of the official languages of the European Community. It must be completed in the language of the country of refund.

Complete the form in BLOCK LETTERS starting each entry at the beginning of the line or space provided. Do not use punctuation marks (full stops, commas etc) unless essential.

In those sections which are marked ⌶—⌶—⌶—⌶—⌶ do not insert more than one character (letter, figure, punctuation marks etc). Recognised abbreviations may be used (eg 'Ltd' for Limited).

The application must be submitted by 30th June of the year following that to which the application relates. Applications may be submitted if the conditions set out in the notes to Boxes 4 & 5 are met. The application must be made to the competent authority of the state of refund, viz:

Belgium
Bureau Central de TVA pour assujettis étrangers,
rue Van Orley 15, 1000 Brussels

Denmark
Toldvaesenets Faelles Opgaver (TFO)
Strandgade 100, DK-1401 Copenhagen K.
Telephone: (0:0 45) 0154 1344

France
Direction Générale des Impôts,
Centre des Non-résidents, 9 Rue d'Uzès,
75084 Paris Cedex 02,
Telephone: (010 33) 1 4004 0404

Germany
Bundesamt für Finanzen,
Postfach 20 03 89, D5300 Bonn 2.
Telephone (010 49) 228 4060

Italy
Ufficio Provinciale Imposta sul Valore Aggiunta,
Via Tolstoi 5, 0144 Roma.

Luxembourg
Administration de l'Enregistrement et des Domaines,
Bureau d'Imposition 10, 12 Rue d'Epernay,
BP 1004 Luxembourg (Grand Duché).
Telephone: (010 352) 477 1521

Republic of Ireland
The Revenue Commissioners,
VAT Repayments Section, Castle House,
Sth. Great George's Street, Dublin 2.
Telephone: (00) 01 792777

The Netherlands
de Inspecteur der invoerrechten en accijnzen,
Postbus 5408, 2280 H. K. Rijswijk
Telephone: (010 31 70) 725811.

The United Kingdom
H M Customs and Excise,
VAT Control Division C (Branch 3), St. John's House,
Merton Road, Liverpool L20 3NN.
Telephone: 051 922 6393

B. Tax Reference number

The number to be inserted in the box in the top left-hand corner of the claim will be issued by the competent authority in the state of refund, so leave it blank on your first claim to any member state.

You will be notified of your reference number, which may be different in each state, for use with second or subsequent claims. Please ensure that you use the correct number or leave the box blank.

C. Numbered boxes.

Box 1. Your name and address will be shown on all communications sent to you exactly as you write it on the form.

Box 2. State the type of business activity engaged in during the period of the claim.

Box 3. The application must be accompanied by a certificate of status issued by the official authority of the state in which you are established to provide evidence that you are a taxable person for the purpose of VAT in that state. However, where the competent authority of the state in which the claim is to be made already holds such evidence, you are not bound to produce another status certificate for a period of one year from the date of issue of the first certificate.

Box 4. The application should refer to purchase of goods or services invoiced, or imports made, during a period of not less than three months or more than one calendar year. However, it may relate to a period of less than three months where the period represents the end of a calendar year. Claims may also include invoices or import documents not covered by previous applications and concerning transactions made during the calendar year in question.

Box 5. The application may be used for more than one invoice or import document. If the period to which the claim relates is three months or more, but less than one calendar year (January–December), the total amount of VAT claimed must not be less than:

Belgium	Denmark	France	Germany	Italy
Bfrs 8000	DKr 1500	Ffrs 1200	DM 500	LIT 250,000

Otherwise, if the period is one calendar year or the remainder of a calendar year, the amount of VAT claimed must not be less than:

Bfrs 1000	DKr 200	Ffrs 160	DM 60	LIT 35,000

Luxembourg	Republic of Ireland	Netherlands	United Kingdom
Lfrs 8000	£130	FL 550	£130

Otherwise, if the period is one calendar year or the remainder of a calendar year, the amount of VAT claimed must not be less than:

Lfrs 1000	£16	FL 70	£16

Box 6. Do not make any entry in this box.

Box 7. Account number – insert the number of the account to which refund is to be made.

Code number of financial body – insert Sorting Code number of the bank where the account is held. (In the United Kingdom this number is shown in the top right hand corner of the cheque.)

Account in the name of – insert the name of the account holder to whom the refund is to be made.

Name and address of financial body– insert the name and address of the bank where the account is held.

NB. member states reserve the right to make refunds addressed to the applicant.

Box 8. Please attach ORIGINALS of documents showing amount of VAT incurred. The competent authority will stamp each document and provided the claim is satisfactory return them within 1 month of receipt.

Box 9(a). Describe nature of activities for which goods acquired or services received mentioned in the application for refund of tax

eg Participated in

International...............................Fair, held in...........................

from........................to...........................Stand No. ....

OR

International carriage of goods as

from.....................to.......................on.........................

If insufficient space is available you must use a continuation sheet, headed with your tax registration number, endorsed 'Box 9(a)' and attached firmly to the application form.

Box 9(b). Exempted transport services are those carried out in connection with the international carriage of goods, including – subject to certain conditions – transport services associated with the transit, export or import of goods.

Box 9(c). Any refund which is obtained improperly may render the offender liable to the fines or penalties laid down by the law of the state which has made the refund.

Appendix 2

Guidance for completion of the UK application form

Tax reference number

The number to be inserted in the box in the top left hand corner of the claim form will be issued by the competent authority in the state of refund, so it should be left blank on the first claim to any Member State. You will be notified of your reference number, which may be different in each state, for use with second or subsequent claims. The correct number should then be inserted in this box.

Numbered boxes

The application must be completed in block capitals, starting from the left. The application must be completed in the language of the country from which you are claiming.

Other points

Claims may include invoices or import documents not covered by previous applications and concerning transactions made during the calendar year in question.

The application may be used for more than one invoice or import document.

Under the heading 'box 9(a)' the nature of the activities for which you have acquired the goods or received the services mentioned in the application for refund of the tax must be described. If insufficient space is available you should use a continuation sheet, headed with your tax registration number, endorsed 'box 9(a)' and attached firmly to the application form.

The exempted transport services referred to at box 9(b) are those carried out in connection with the international carriage of goods, including – subject to certain conditions – transport services associated with the transit, export or import of goods.

Each document submitted should be consecutively numbered starting with '1'. The number should be inserted in the top right-hand corner of the face of the document.

When tax is incurred by taxable persons who receive VAT group treatment the group representative member must apply on behalf of all the members. As the supporting invoices produced will not necessarily be addressed to the representative member the status certificate must also contain the names of those group members who incurred the tax.

Appendix 3

European community: Territorial limits

For VAT purposes, the territory of the EC is as follows:

- Belgium
- Denmark (excluding Greenland)
- Federal Republic of Germany (excluding the Island of Heligoland and the territory of Busingen)
- France (excluding the overseas territories)
- Greece
- The Republic of Ireland
- Italy (excluding Livigno, Campione d'Italia and the Italian waters of Lake Lugano)
- Luxembourg
- Netherlands
- Portugal
- Spain
- United Kingdom.

For VAT purposes, the following territories are not in the EC:

- The Channel Islands
- Andorra
- Liechtenstein
- Monaco: however Monaco operates a VAT refund system as if it were a Member State. Please refer to the BDO office at P O Box 159, Monte-Carlo, MC 98000, tel: 93-301515 for further details.
- San Marino
- The Vatican

For UK VAT purposes the Isle of Man is treated as part of the UK.

Transactions with the Channel Islands and the continental shelf outside UK territorial waters, for example oil rigs, are imports and exports. Imports and exports do not arise between Great Britain and Northern Ireland nor between the UK and the Isle of Man.

1 United Kingdom
2 Republic of Ireland
3 Portugal
4 Spain
5 France
6 Belgium

7 Luxembourg
8 Netherlands
9 Denmark
10 Germany
11 Italy
12 Greece

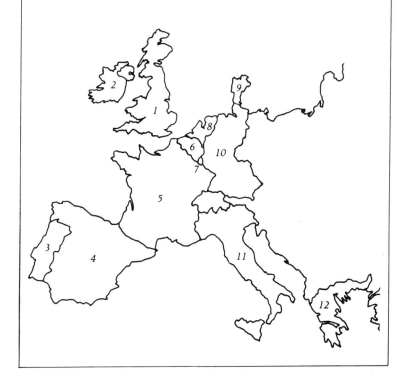

Index